MOMS ON CALL

Basic Baby Care:
0-6 Months

D1319522

Laura Hunter, LPN and
Jennifer Walker, RN, BSN

Printed in the United States of America
ISBN 978-0-9854114-2-8

Editing by Tim Walker
Cover photo by Alice Park Photography
Cover design and logo design by Kristen Smith and Alice Park
Family photo on back cover by Alice Park Photography

Published in the United States by
Moms on Call, LLC
5200 Dallas Hwy Ste 200 #226
Powder Springs, GA 30127

(Left to right -Jennifer Walker RN BSN and Laura Hunter LPN)

About the Authors

Laura Hunter (LPN)

Laura is a mother of five, a pediatric nurse with over 20 years of experience, an entrepreneur, and a highly sought after infant-care consultant who has an international following. But there's one common passion for all the areas of Laura's life—her desire to inspire and encourage parents.

Jennifer Walker (RN BSN)

Jennifer has multiple roles—wife, mother of three, pediatric nurse, public speaker, infant and toddler care consultant and author. Jennifer has over 20 years of pediatric nursing experience and has a heart to equip parents with practical advice and inspiration for the joys and challenges of parenthood.

Moms on Call LLC is an Atlanta-based phenomenon. We started serving local families with in-home parenting consultations from birth to 4 years of age. And now, by combining technology, common sense and a passion for families, we have supported and partnered with parents all over the globe. Our books, swaddling blankets, online resources and seminars are all available at momsoncall.com.

"This book is dedicated to the living God who guides our paths and makes every day an exciting adventure."
- Jennifer and Laura

Seeking medical care whenever you are concerned is recommended by Moms on Call.

Any time that you are concerned, or notice any symptoms, call your pediatrician's office. Sometimes babies have discreet symptoms like a fever and at other times there is just something that you can't explain; call it mother's intuition or a nagging feeling that something may be wrong. Those are both valid reasons to seek medical attention. Many of the concepts addressed in this book vary from pediatrician to pediatrician. When it comes to your child's care, you are responsible for making the final decisions.

This book is designed to provide information on the care of babies up to 6 months of age. This book is intended as a reference volume only, not as a medical manual. It is sold with the understanding that neither the author nor the publisher are engaged in rendering medical, health, or any other kind of personal professional services in the book. The reader should consult the services of a competent pediatrician, registered dietician or other medical professional. The author and publisher specifically disclaim all responsibility for any liability, loss, or risk, personal or otherwise, to any parent, person, or entity with respect to any illness, disability, injury, loss or damage to be caused, or alleged to be caused, directly or indirectly, of the use and/or application of any of the contents of this book.

The book should be used only as a supplement to your pediatrician's advice, not as a substitute for it. It is not the purpose of this book to replace the regular care of, or contradict the advice from, the

American Academy of Pediatrics, or any pediatrician, nutritionist, registered dietician, or other professional person or organization. This text should be used only as a general guide and should not be considered an ultimate source of childcare, child rearing, sleep training techniques, child feeding, food preparation/storage, or as the ultimate source of any other information. You are urged to read other available information and learn as much as possible about childcare and the nutrition and feeding of young children. For more information, see the references at the back of this book. Mention of specific companies, organizations, or authorities in this book does not imply endorsement by the publisher, nor does mention of specific companies, organizations, or authorities imply that they endorse this book.

Every reasonable effort has been made to make this book as complete and as accurate as possible. However, there may be mistakes, both typographical and in content. Therefore, this text should be used as only a general guide. You should discuss with your pediatrician the information contained in this book before applying it. This book contains information only up to the copyright date. New information, or information contradicting that which is found in this book, should be actively sought from your child's competent medical professionals.

TESTIMONIALS

"I just wanted to let you know that Haley has been sleeping from 10:00 p.m. until 5:00 a.m. almost every night, then she goes back to bed until 7:00 a.m. We are so thankful!!! We will certainly pass it along to EVERYONE we know." —Tina & Drew B.

"Paine is now 10 weeks and the good news is he has been sleeping through the night for a few weeks now!" —Heather S.

"The confidence she has in what she does has helped my husband and I feel that confidence with our own child. It is my wish that every expectant parent whom you encounter reads this right away!" —Hope H.

"I still can't believe what a miracle worker you are. I tell everyone we wouldn't have made it without you (or at least we would have been very sleep deprived). He sleeps 12 hours a night. What a lifesaver!! I just flip through your book for the answers. I think just showing us that all it really takes is a lot of love and a little discipline has helped guide us." —Karin S.

"It was unbelievable how rested she was the next day. That swaddle really helped her to sleep! She was so calm and happy, like a different baby altogether." —Katherine C.

"James' naps are going SO well. Now he almost always plays in his crib quietly when he wakes up, and takes wonderful long naps in the morning, and solid, shorter ones in the afternoon. Hooray! Thank you, thank you!" —Elisabeth I.

Table of Contents

FOREWORD

Hello! We are Laura Hunter LPN and Jennifer Walker RN BSN, two moms and pediatric nurses who decided it was time to write a how-to childcare book that moms could really use—a book by moms and for moms that addressed reality. No psychobabble, not the exhaustive book of disorders that could cause immediate anxiety in the calmest of mothers. No—something different. Something we knew moms needed.

How did we know? Well, between us, we are raising 8 children: two girls (thank you Laura), two sets of twin boys and two singleton boys. We did so without nannies or night-nurses (although my mother-in-law was a life-saver – Jen). Now, the clincher here is what we did to help earn enough money to be home during the day to enjoy each and every sloppy meal and stay home at night to snuggle up to whichever child had the current virus that was going around the school.

As we mentioned, we are pediatric nurses. Not only pediatric nurses, but nurses on call. When the busy 9,000-patient pediatric office was closed and moms had questions after hours, they paged us. So from 5 p.m. to 8:30 a.m. every weekday and all weekend, the pager went off. Every worry and need that any mom was experiencing about her child, be it medical or otherwise . . . we answered.

After about the 300th call about basic infant care, Laura decided she had to do something better to help teach these new moms how to care for their infants. So, she decided to do in-home infant care consultations. We developed a packet of information and instructions for new parents. Then, Laura went into parents' homes and went over the materials that we developed, helping parents to get their babies to sleep, and educating them

11

on common infant care issues. After the first consult, we knew that this is what God had purposed in our hearts. Testimonial after testimonial from pleased parents came pouring in. Every consult we did resulted in success story after success story and with no marketing at all, Moms on Call grew 600% over the first three years.

So, here we are as the result of the popular demand for the real story. Together, we developed this need-to-know manual that shares the realities of parenting.

Laura and I have answered thousands of questions from moms. We know what moms worry about at 9 a.m. We know what moms worry about at 4 p.m. We know what moms worry about at 8 p.m. and we definitely know what moms worry about at 2 in the morning. We know because it was our job to answer questions for many years, and we know because we have our own children. We have thought some of the same thoughts, and we have felt some of the same feelings. We know what moms worry about because we are moms.

There is a common fear of doing the wrong thing or making the wrong choice. When a baby is born, it is like a new part of your heart blossomed that you never knew was even there. This concept is impossible to explain; it can only be felt. We have been there. I (Jennifer) was so nervous with baby #1 (Grayson) that it was all I could do to leave him in the care of his incredibly capable and loving grandmother.

So, we have felt the sting of leaving baby #1 to go to work. That first day is a heartbreaker, and we suffered through it. By the time both of our twins came along, working outside the home was no longer a feasible option. Taking calls from home was a great compromise. Difficult, yes, but it has allowed us to interact with other moms in a way only another mom

12

can, with a heart of compassion and understanding.

We did *not* do everything "right" with all our kids. We learned along the way, just like everyone else. We learned about the reality of parenting. And we, too, read the popular baby books. We got particularly frustrated when the advice assumed that there was only one child in the household, or that parents only have to deal with one child at a time. Most of the books left us feeling overwhelmed. It seemed as if they promised some instant fix that never came. So, if you are looking for a false sense of perfection, you will not find it here. What you will hopefully find here is a succinct, easy-to-read reference guide.

Children are amazing and wonderful creatures, full of mysteries and wonder. We desire to use our experience and education to help you enjoy the treasure or treasures that God has so graciously given you. He thought you were the best parent for this child/children. You may not have a degree or even a good role model, but He chose you. We want to help equip you with some of the information that we know moms need. This book will not make you a perfect parent, but perhaps we can help you enjoy the ride.

Receiving instruction about basic baby care can help decrease parental anxieties. However, there is so much more to learn, each and every day. We truly have a heart for parents, moms in particular. The information in this book has helped so many parents enjoy and understand their babies as evidenced by the glowing testimonials (remember, they are simply enjoying the parenting process better). We have not magically made them perfect parents. With that in mind, may this journey bless and enrich your life.

For more Moms On Call resources, please go to
www.momsoncall.com

More than 175,000 books sold:
Moms On Call: Basic Baby Care (0-6 months)
Moms On Call: Next Steps Baby Care (6-15 months)
Moms On Call: Toddler Book

PARENTING RESOURCES: NEWBORN - 4 YEARS OF AGE

Online Classes:
- Three comprehensive online courses
- Dozens of complimentary videos
- Available via multiple platforms to meet families where they are

One-on-One Consultations:
- In-home consultations
- Virtual consultations
- On-Going Email Support
- Network of Trained Consultants

Mobile Apps (IOS/Android):
- Moms On Call Scheduler
- Moms On Call Toddler by Design

Products:
- The Official Moms On Call Swaddle Blanket
- More to come!

SECTION ONE: THE BASICS

What Every Mom and Dad Need To Know About Basic Infant Care

"Keep sound wisdom and discretion; so they will be life to your soul and grace to your neck."
Proverbs 3:21b-22

GENERAL SHOPPING LIST

Moms on Call recommends having the following items on hand prior to needing them. This will cut down on any middle of the night trips to the pharmacy after you speak to the pediatrician's office.

These items are the ones that we have in our own closets. So, if you want to know what two pediatric nurses with eight kids keep in the medicine cabinet, this is it! These items can be found at momsoncall.com.

Note: Do not administer any medications to your baby without consulting your pediatrician.

MEDICINE CABINET

- Liquid acetaminophen (2-3 bottles)
- Acetaminophen suppositories
- Diphenhydramine liquid (2-3 bottles)
- Normal saline nose drops (plain saline)
- Glycerin suppositories
- Pedialyte® (electrolyte replenisher)
- Pedialyte® popsicles
- Digital thermometer (2-3)
- Vaseline®
- Medicine dosage syringes
- Infant gas drops

DIAPER RASH ITEMS

- Vitamin A&D Ointment® (without zinc oxide)
- Lotrimin AF® (may find in foot care section of the pharmacy)
- Cocoa Butter cream
- Aqua-Phor Healing Ointment®
- Regular kitchen corn starch
- Kirkland Diaper Wipes®

SKIN CARE

- Aveeno Oatmeal Bath Packets®
- Eucerin® or Lubriderm® lotion
- Neutrogena T-gel® shampoo (to be applied as instructed in the book for cradle cap with the approval of the pediatrician—not for regular use)

FIRST AID KIT

- Hydrocortisone 0.5% cream
- Hydrogen peroxide (2-3 smaller bottles)
- Polysporin Antibiotic Ointment®
- Antibacterial hand wash
- 4x4 Gauze - individually packed (2-3 boxes)
- 2x2 Gauze individually packed (2-3 boxes)
- Band-Aids® (flexible fabric)
- Ace bandages (2-3 rolls)
- Squeezable ice packs
- Tweezers (diagonal head) (2-3)
- Medical tape

MISC.

- Baby pear or white grape juice
- Canned peaches in heavy syrup
- Children's bug repellent (Spray on hands, then apply to child sparingly, or just put repellent on baby's clothes and socks and a squirt on the stroller/car seat prior to placing baby in it.)
- Sunscreen (our favorites come in a stick for ease of facial application.)
- Nail clippers by Safety First® (with the white handgrip)
- Long handled infant spoons (usually one piece of plastic)
- Biz laundry soap (Great for stain removal—especially if items are soaked overnight then washed in a regular laundry cycle.)

> **Note:** Remember to always keep a digital thermometer, a bottle of acetaminophen and a bottle of children's diphenhydramine secured in your diaper bag.

BABY SHOWER LIST

Baby's Room
- o Moms on Call Swaddle Blankets 2-3 momsoncall.com.
- o Nail clippers with the white handgrip
- o Crib (bought new or within the past 5 years)
- o Firm crib mattress (bought new or within the past 5 years)
- o Breathable mesh bumper pad -1 (Optional)
- o Crib sheets 4-6
- o Short sleeve onesie 10
- o Light cotton sleeper with footies 6-8
- o Video monitor
- o Sound Machine (made for adults)
- o Plug covers (they even make ones that cover outlets where things are plugged in)
- o Cool mist humidifier for use as needed
- o Carbon monoxide and smoke detector

Bathroom
- o Baby hair and body wash
- o Washcloths 6-8 baby size, 2-3 regular
- o Adult sized towels 4-6
- o Hand towels 2-4
- o Baby brush with medium bristles
- o Anti-skid mat for the bottom of the tub

Changing Stations
- Bulb syringe (keep the one they give you at the hospital)
- Kirkland's Diaper Wipes® (Costco)
- Changing pad (you can put rug grippers or velcro tape underneath the changing pad where it touches the dresser to help keep it from slipping)
- Changing pad covers 4-6
- Diapers (Pampers Swaddlers are our favorite for babies under 12 pounds)
- Digital thermometer -2 (one for the diaper bag)
- Basket with the recommended diaper rash items from the "General Shopping List"

Feeding
- Gerber First Essentials or Similac disposable nipples (Amazon®) on standard bottles- 9 (Five oz. Bottles) and 9 (Nine oz. bottles)
- Bottle brush to clean inside of bottles
- Breastfeeding pillow
- Regular adult pillows to prop behind your back and under your breastfeeding pillow for support
- Breast pump (you can rent this from the hospital, you will want the electric one)
- Long handled infant spoons 6-8
- Small bowls 6-8
- Formula (you will get samples from the hospital)
- Breast milk storage bags
- Spill-proof sippy cups - 4

General
- Bouncy seat (get two if you a have a 2 story house)
- Car seat (new with additional bases for all caregivers' vehicles)
- Baby swing
- Stroller (light enough for you to manage)
- Pacifiers (because the BEST ones are often hard to find, see the link at momsoncall.com)
- Cloth diapers 6-8 (to catch the spit-up when we burp the baby)
- Standard baby blankets 3-4 (for tummy time on the floor, putting over them in the car seat/bouncy seat or swing)
- Age appropriate baby toys are great but in the first six months, the most fun and interesting thing in the world is you!

Optional items we will **not** need
- Baby comforter (no loose blankets in the crib)
- Baby plastic bathtub (we will wash the baby in the big person bathtub)
- Diaper wipe warmer (we like the wipes to be refreshingly cool)
- Breast-like nipples for bottles (old-fashioned style nipples work best in our vast experience)
- Mobile (Babies learn by association. We want them to associate crib with sleep time, not playtime.)

BATHING

For a bathing routine demonstration, see momsoncall.com. Your baby likely will have their first bath at home. It is unbelievably fun and adorable! Support baby's head until he/she can do so on their own. Always make sure that all supplies are kept within arm's reach. A basket of items is an easy way to ensure that everything is kept together.

Until the umbilical cord falls off:

- Wash the baby's face with warm water and a washcloth (slightly warmer than room temperature).
- Clean diaper area thoroughly with Kirkland's wipes or unscented alcohol-free wipes.
- Put fresh clothes or pajamas on them.
- This does not have to be a big production.
- After the umbilical cord falls off, regular baths may be given. (Baby soap is optional but it sure makes them smell good!)

After Umbilical Cord Falls Off

Prior to bath

- Clean the genitals at the changing table
- Females—Do not wash female genital areas with soap. Soap is irritating to those parts.
- You may notice white, cheesy-looking stuff in the crevices. That is normal. It is just sloughed skin that mixes with the natural moisture in that area.

Tip: Spread the labia (lip-like parts) and clean with a diaper wipe or washcloth FRONT TO BACK, so as not to introduce any stool into the urethra where the urine comes out. This will help us avoid bladder infections. You only have to get this thorough of a cleaning once a day, PRIOR to the bath.

- Males (circumcised)—After the circumcision is healed, gently pull skin back so the head of the penis is seen all the way around and clean well. Sometimes, some diaper cream or stool gets between the skin folds around the circumcised area so this will help us to keep it clean.
- Males (uncircumcised)—Clean the foreskin. There is no need to retract the skin. Speak with your doctor for specific care.

Bath Routine

- Once the umbilical cord falls off, bathe every evening as a matter of routine. Babies learn by association and they will associate bath time with bedtime.
- Things to have at arm's reach in the bathroom
    - Washcloths
    - Baby wash/shampoo
    - Soft baby brush
    - Bouncy seat (placed near the tub, not in the tub)
- Fill the tub with 5-6 inches of warm water.
- We use the adult bathtub because it keeps the water warm and relaxes the baby.
- Place an adult-sized towel in the bouncy seat next to (not in) the tub and place the baby on top of the towel—strap them in. This is our "docking

station," so-to-speak.
- o Kneel down next to the tub. Put the soap bottle right into the bath for easy access.
- o Grasp the baby in a C-hold behind the head and neck and with your other hand scoop them right between the legs so that your fingers are splayed beneath their buttocks. Your thumb and forefinger can then easily wrap around the upper thigh. This hold is very secure and allows you to transfer the baby into the tub with ease.
- o They may cry momentarily as they get used to the water. This is fine, they will settle down.
- o Once the baby's bottom is resting against the bottom of the tub, remove the hand that was under their bottom and use that hand to take a washcloth, dip it in the warm water and cover their little midsection with it so they remain warm.
- o As you are bent over the tub, place your body weight (just below your ribcage) on the side of the tub to support your back.
- o The hand behind their head and neck will stay in position to support the baby's head and neck.
- o The free hand will dispense the soap onto the washcloth (which is on their tummy) as an easy access point to get the soap needed for use on the baby's arms, legs, torso and head.
- o We clean the head last so that their head does not get cold.
- o Dispense the baby wash directly onto the bristles of the baby brush and then scrub that little scalp. This dislodges any dry skin that can mix with the oil in the scalp and cause cradle cap.
- o You will not hurt that soft spot with the baby brush so give them a good scrub.

- Rinse their head by scooping some water into your hand and gently rinsing their scalp with bathwater. Try to avoid getting it in their face.
- Then we are done and ready to scoop our hand between their legs, under that bottom and lift them back out of the tub into the awaiting towel that is resting on the bouncy seat.
- Let the water out of the tub, stand up and *then* you can take the baby wrapped in that soft towel, back to their room to get into their jammies.
- Never leave your baby/babies in the tub or around water unattended.

Umbilical Cord Care: Keep cord dry. You can clean around the edges with a Q-Tip® dipped in regular rubbing alcohol to clean the dried blood (the dried blood is left over maternal blood from the umbilical cord).

It will look almost like the inside of a steamed oyster (sorry) for the first week. It may have an end that looks like dried fruit.

Call the pediatrician if you notice:

- Strong foul odor (trust us, it finds you).

- Bleeding - More than one teaspoon of bright red blood that runs out of the belly-button. (Dried blood is okay. If the cord has bright red or even persistent dried blood, the pediatrician can usually fix it by putting on a special compound that is painless for baby.)

- Oozing yellow/whitish discharge.

BOWEL MOVEMENTS

"My baby is three weeks old and has not had a stool for almost 24 hours!!!"

Can you believe how we obsess over our baby's bowel movements? Color, consistency, frequency and amount of apparent straining are common concerns for moms. Let us set your mind at ease. There is a wide range of what is considered normal for a bowel movement.

After the first week of life, if you are lucky, bowel movements slow down from every feeding to maybe once or twice a day, and even once a week for some two and three month olds (If you are not lucky, your twins have simultaneous and copious stools eight times a day each until they are three years old. That's sixteen poopy diapers per day between them! - Jennifer)

Color
- o Breastfed: generally yellow seedy; can vary from yellowish brown to green
- o Formula fed: darker in color; can vary from yellow to brown to green

Frequency
- o Breastfed or formula fed: May vary greatly.
- o The first 2-3 weeks, the baby may be stooling every feeding, from small amounts to full diapers.
- o However, by the time your baby/babies reach 2-3 weeks old, they may stool as frequently as every feeding or as infrequently as once a week. What a difference!

Consistency
- May go from watery to semi-soft
- There is a digestive change around 6-8 weeks of age. You may notice a change in consistency, frequency, gas and amount of straining. This lasts about a week and then the stools become more predictable.

> **Note:** Remember, babies commonly grunt, push, strain, draw up their legs and turn red in the face when they are passing a stool. This is normal. They are just getting the hang of what muscles to clench in order to move the stool and gas. Think about what you would do if you had to have a bowel movement while lying down. It may look painful but it is not. It is all a part of normal growth and development and learning how to produce a stool.

Call pediatrician's office if:
- More than 1 teaspoon bright red blood at any time
- Less than 1 teaspoon bright red blood for 3 or more stools
- Black, tarry stools
- What looks like coffee grounds
- Clay (gray or beige) colored stool for more than 2 weeks

CONSTIPATION

True constipation is a term used to describe hard, pebble-like stools. There is a difference between constipation and infrequent stooling. Infrequent stoolers are gassy and have a large, **soft** bowel movement every 3-7 days.

Signs of Constipation
- o Painful passage of stools when the stool itself is hard and pebble-like
- o Abdomen is distended but remains relatively soft
- o Decreased appetite

Relief measures if your pediatrician diagnoses constipation:
- o In babies, you may stimulate a bowel movement with a rectal thermometer or Q-Tip® with Vaseline®. Insert ¼ inch into the rectum and rotate Q-Tip® a few times. Rectal stimulation can be used every other day only if uncomfortable. If you have to do this for longer than 2 weeks, consult your pediatrician.
- o For babies over 4 weeks of age: we can add an ounce of juice in the morning and an optional ounce in the afternoon with the approval of the pediatrician to help naturally soften those stools. (Use Gerber pear or white grape juice by mouth in a bottle until stool consistency is soft, no longer than 3 days.)

o Glycerin suppository OTC (over the counter). If you have to use these for longer than 2 weeks, consult your pediatrician.
o Babies more than 4 months old (on baby foods) may have baby food, such as apricots, prunes, peaches, pears, plums, beans, peas, or spinach at least 2 times per day. Avoid carrots, squash, rice, and bananas for 3-4 days.
o Your pediatrician can recommend a stool softener to be taken for approximately a week. However, stool softeners are generally not used in babies under six months old.

> **Note:** True constipation is when you see hard, pebble-like stools.

When to seek medical care
o No relief after trying above
o Abdominal tenderness (baby cries) when pressing on either side of the abdomen at the level of the belly button (Make sure your hands are not too cold!)
o Rectal temperature in a baby under 3 months of age over 100.4° F
o Fever over 101.5° F in a baby over 3 months of age
o Happens frequently
o Persistent vomiting (See vomiting section)

INFREQUENT STOOLERS

Signs
- Soft stools: can be every other day to once every 7 days! That is a wide range for what is considered normal.
- May have increased gas and/or fussiness
- This is not something that needs to be treated: It is how a baby is designed. They just stool infrequently but the stool remains soft.

Relief measures for infrequent stoolers: (Only if the baby seems uncomfortable and with the approval of your pediatrician):
- Rectal stimulation can be used every other day only if uncomfortable. If you have to do this for longer than 2 weeks, consult your pediatrician.
- For babies over 4 weeks of age, we can add an ounce of juice in the morning and an optional ounce in the afternoon with the approval of the pediatrician to help produce stools. (Use Gerber pear or white grape juice by mouth in a bottle for up to 3-4 days.)
- Infant gas drops

Note: Infrequent stooling is not a problem and does not have to be treated. It is perfectly normal for many babies and toddlers.

NAIL CLIPPING

For a nail clipping demonstration see momsoncall.com.

Trimming the nails right after a feeding or after bathing is best. Use nail clippers that have a white handgrip pictured at momsoncall.com— they are easiest to maneuver.

- Do this when NO ONE is watching you.
- Place the infant on your lap with their back against your chest and their legs on either side of one of your legs.
- Do not be afraid to hold the baby firmly. You will not squeeze their fingers off; they are going to be fine.
- They may cry through this whole process and that is not unusual or harmful to them in any way.
- Use the corner of the nail clippers to slide the nail clipper under the nail.
- When cutting **fingernails**, round off corners to minimize the chance of your infant scratching him or herself.
- You do not have to do all 10 fingernails at once.
- Trim **toenails** straight across to prevent ingrown toenails.
- Clip nails every 1-2 weeks and toenails every 2-3 months.

SKIN CARE

"My baby has these pink bumps on her face and chest, no fever, and she acts fine and we have pictures scheduled for tomorrow."

It is very seldom that you see a child with perfect skin. Expect skin rashes. The pediatrician may diagnose your baby with one of these common skin rashes.

TYPES OF COMMON SKIN RASHES

Baby acne: small red bumps on face, chest, scalp and back. Usually begins at 2-4 weeks and can last until 4-6 months.
   o   Clean with warm water and a washcloth, no need to use soap, lotions or baby oils. Can come and go for several weeks.

Milia: tiny white bumps that occur on the face, nose, forehead, chin, and cheeks. Usually will disappear by 1-2 months of age.

   o   Do not apply any ointments or creams to these.

Drool Rash: pink splotchy area on the chin or cheeks that comes and goes. Can be caused by spitting up, pacifiers that hold drool against skin, or frequent drooling.
   o   Rinse baby's face with water after feedings.
   o   Apply Vaseline® to area to protect skin from irritation.

Wet moist areas: under neck, in skin folds. May use cornstarch to help with moisture.

Cradle Cap: oily yellow scales on scalp. Begins first few weeks of life and can last several weeks.

- o To help prevent cradle cap, shampoo hair with soap and scrub with soft infant brush. Rinse well.
- o If already present, wash hair with Neutrogena T-gel® if approved by your pediatrician. (Remember to keep out of eyes) Apply to hair and scrub lightly with infant hairbrush. Do this 3 times a week. Once clear, use mild infant soap for shampooing. Do not use T-gel for more than 2 weeks. If symptoms last longer than 2 weeks or worsen with treatment then the baby needs to be seen by the pediatrician.
- o If severe crustiness, put some baby oil on the scalp one hour before washing to soften the crust. Make sure to rinse well.

Heat rash: pin-prickly pink bumps and splotchy areas. Can be seen on skin that touches mom's skin during breastfeeding or along the back where baby sweats in the car seat.
- o Change your baby's position during feeding.
- o Apply regular kitchen cornstarch (not baby powder) to back or chest. Put cornstarch in your hand first, and then apply to affected areas. Be careful not to get the powder or the dispenser near the baby's face, as infants can choke on the powder.

Dry flaky skin:
- May use Eucerin® or Lubriderm® to moisturize skin. Dry patches may occur behind knees and elbows, although it may also appear in other areas such as diaper area, or face.
- In the first month of life you may notice dry areas at the ankles, feet and wrists and even on the arms and legs. Babies have a coating over their skin while in the womb called 'vernix'. It sloughs off over the first month of life and looks like dry skin but the lotions do not get rid of it. Just use the washcloth in the bath to gently rub it off.

Note: Any blisters containing clear fluid or pimples containing pus which occur in the first month of life, or any rash accompanied by a fever must be seen by the Pediatrician.

Diaper rash
See the Moms on Call instructions for diaper rash on our website, momsoncall.com.

- **Redness.** Leave open to air (for as long as is practical!). May use diaper cream (Vitamin A&D®, Aquaphor®, Cocoa Butter). Also, may use kitchen cornstarch to keep moisture from irritating the skin. Change diapers frequently.

- **Red and bumpy.** Leave open to air (again, for as long as is practical). Change frequently. Apply Lotrimin AF® three times a day if approved by your pediatrician. Follow with any diaper cream listed above and kitchen cornstarch. Use for 7 days. If there is bleeding or no improvement in 3-4 days, then see your pediatrician.

Tip: Laura likes to use a combination of Aqua-Phor® and Cocoa Butter mixed together, then apply cornstarch. We also recommend Kirkland Diaper Wipes® (at Costco). You can also buy these in bulk, which is good because you will use more than you think.

Note: You can see a diaper changing demonstration at momsoncall.com.

ORAL CARE/TEETHING

"My child is so fussy. I am wondering if she is teething or has an ear infection?"

There is no way to definitively tell whether or not your baby has an ear infection unless the doctor looks in the ear. However, teething can begin as early as 2-3 months or as late as one year old. (Jennifer—My children had no teeth until they were about 11 months old. They discovered the joy of gumming everything from Cheerios to cheese!) Some children do not have any pain while teething. And we all hope for that kind of child!

Signs
- Increased drooling
- Chewing constantly
- Swollen, red gums

Relief Measures
- Wet an infant washcloth slightly and put it in the freezer for 10 minutes. Allow them to chew on it as needed – supervised of course.
- Place a saline-filled teether in the fridge for 10-20 minutes and then let them chew on it.

Note: It is very difficult to tell the difference between teething and ear pain. If running a fever more than 2-3 days, not sleeping well, grabbing at ears or has cold symptoms, call your pediatrician.

Dental Care once teeth erupt
- Begin brushing teeth/gums with wet gauze or washcloth wrapped around your index finger. Be careful not to let the gauze slip off your finger.
- Never allow your child to go to sleep with milk/formula residue on their gums/teeth. This causes painful tooth decay. **That means no bottles in the crib!**

The first visit to the dentist should be around 2-3 years old, but it can be earlier if there is noticeable tooth decay or problems, including chipped teeth.

Thrush: White irregular shaped patches that coat the inside of the mouth and sometimes the tongue (if only on tongue may not be thrush). The coating cannot be wiped off with your fingernail. May cause mild discomfort when eating. Call office if you suspect thrush.

- Nystatin oral suspension can usually be called into the pharmacy if your doctor's office suspects thrush.
- Boil all bottle nipples and pacifiers for 5 minutes each night during treatment. Also wipe down baby toys that come in contact with the mouth with a cloth and rinse thoroughly. Do this for the first three days of treatment.
- If breastfeeding, apply Nystatin to irritated areas of nipples with your OB/GYN's approval. Also clean your nipples with vinegar washes after every feeding and let air

dry (one part vinegar to two parts water i.e. one teaspoon of vinegar mixed with two teaspoons of water).

When to seek medical care

- o If no improvement after doing Nystatin for 7 days.
- o The thrush gets worse instead of better.
- o Discomfort continues after doing treatment for 3-4 days.

CRYING

"I hate to hear my baby cry, for any reason at any time."

Normal Behavior
- o Good parents have babies that cry sometimes. It is part of how they communicate and learn.
- o 10-15 minute segments of crying **especially in the evening** is expected.
- o Starting at about 2-4 weeks of age, they can be fed, changed, and in the loving arms of a parent and cry like you are trying to pull off an arm.
- o Babies have a startle reflex that comes from out of nowhere and they do not know how to control their arms or legs. This can get frustrating by the end of the day.
- o Babies have a certain amount of energy that they have to release. And until they develop some more muscle mass, crying is the only way they can get rid of all that energy.
- o Once they can sit up without support and roll over in both directions (about 5-6 months of age to do both) then they have adequate ways of burning off that energy. Until then, evening time is the fussiest time of day.
- o Following the schedules that we outline in this book and establishing great sleep habits will help considerably.
- o As we mentioned above, they may cry *on and off* for 2-3 hours, especially in the evening. We do not want your baby to have more than 2 hours of *inconsolable* crying during the day and we are

not asking you to ignore their basic needs, such as diaper changes and feedings. Just be prepared for babies to cry for no apparent reason in the evenings and 15-20 minute segments during the day. It does not necessarily mean that you are doing something wrong.

Overstimulation
- A baby cannot handle the hustle and bustle of the adult lifestyle. Make sure that all the naps are not in the car or "on the run."
- Be aware of your child's limitations.
- Have at least two naps a day in the crib.

Food Sensitivity
- Babies can be sensitive to different milk varieties (breast or formula), indicated by the following:
  - Severe crying usually after each feeding
  - Forceful vomiting several times per day
  - Watery stools with mucous (looks like snot) or blood-tinged mucous.

Acid Reflux
- All babies have some degree of reflux. There are two kinds of spitters: happy ones (no need for treatment) and unhappy ones (can be treated with medication per the pediatrician).
- Can be a dribble or two after each feeding or forceful vomiting 2-3 times per day
- Crying with meals and at night
- Arching back and frequent interruptions in feeding patterns
- See the chapter entitled "SPITTING UP" for more information

FRUSTRATION

"My baby does not want to roll over"

Children learn by practicing. They do the same thing over and over again. It may take 20-30 times of doing something the right way (or the wrong way) before they consistently do it the right way. Continue to allow them the opportunity to learn. If your child is about to crawl and is crying for a toy across the room, do not get it for him/her/them. Their frustration level can motivate them to achieve developmental milestones.

If we have "tummy time" in the evening, when the baby is already trying to get rid of some extra energy, then the learning process involved in rolling over will be much more successful, because it is fueled by the natural motivator of frustration. We recommend about three sessions of tummy time per day that last 5-10 minutes, even if the baby is fussy.

We also have normal parental frustrations. The constant care of a newborn can be difficult even though we love the baby with all of our heart. This is a demanding time both physically and emotionally. If you are having feelings of despair or find yourself intensely resentful of the baby, it is good to contact your OB/GYN as postpartum depression can come in many forms and is nothing to be embarrassed about. The hormones can be relentless and can have a profound effect on our mental well-being. Seek the help that you need, it is confidential and the treatments can be temporary and effective.

TWINS

"My twins do not sleep at night. We are exhausted!"

Here are the survival tactics that helped us:

1. **If one baby eats, they both eat—period**. Even if one twin does not appear hungry, feed that one anyway. Keep them on the exact same schedule and we mean it! It is okay to put them both in bouncy seats and feed them simultaneously with bottles. Just remember to talk softly to both of them and give them each a few minutes of your full attention. Breast-feeders can hold both babies in the football hold and feed at the same time.

(Jennifer- I did not like the way simultaneous breastfeeding felt and decided to breastfeed one baby and bottle-feed the other on an alternating basis. At each feeding, whomever bottle-fed last time became the breast feeder and the other one got the bottle. I would breastfeed the one baby in the cradle hold while holding a bottle in the other baby's mouth with my "free" hand. The baby with the bottle was generally propped up on a nearby bouncy seat or Boppy® pillow. This way they both were getting at least half of their nutrition from breast milk every day. And they were fed, burped and changed in 45 minutes!)

It is also good to allow Dad to feed the babies sometimes. He can feed both with pumped breast milk from a bottle or formula. It gives Dad a chance to have that much needed interaction.

2. **When one baby sleeps, the other does also. Naptimes and bedtimes are the same.** (See #4 for

specific guidelines for "bedtime.") Again, one baby may not seem sleepy at the same time as the other. This is survival mode. They will learn to be on the same schedule. This is part of learning to live in a family environment. One twin may have to learn to sleep more to accommodate the family schedule. Exception: If one baby wakes 15 minutes earlier from a nap, it is fine to get that baby up a little early.

3. **Use your helpers**. In the first two or three years (honestly), you will be absolutely exhausted. If grandma comes for a visit one day, allow her to watch the babies while you nap for an hour or two. If neighbors or friends ask how they can help, allow them to make a meal or arrange for household chores. Many people would love to help if they just had a tangible thing to do. Let others make meals for you. If someone you trust offers to babysit, say "That sounds great; when are you available?" Think of it this way: the more you allow others to help, the more time you will have to actually enjoy your twins!

4. **Use the Moms on Call Method of getting your babies to sleep.** We do realize that some moms do not have the extra hands around at night. Also, single parents of twins are more likely to have to do the "Bath time" and "Bedtime" routines alone. So, here is a way to do the "Bathtime" and "Bedtime" routines if you are alone.
  - Place a towel over each bouncy seat and place it in the bathroom (one may have to be directly outside the bathroom depending on space available)
  - Put both babies in the bouncy seat in the bathroom and fold the towels over them to keep

them warm. Strap them in.

- Place the loudest baby nearest the bath and use the Moms on Call bathing method outlined at momsoncall.com to transfer baby #1 into the bath. Wash baby #1 and then place baby #1 back in the awaiting towel in the bouncy seat. (Remember to always strap the babies into the bouncy seat at all times.) Then switch the places of the two bouncy seats so that you can repeat the above process with baby #2. They can use the same bathwater, just run a little extra water in the bath for baby #2 so it stays nice and warm.
- Once they are both bathed and both sitting in their towels/bouncy seats, unstrap baby #1 and take that baby (towel and all) to the changing table for lotion and pajamas. When that baby is clothed, return baby #1 to the bouncy seat while you repeat the process with baby #2. Someone may be crying through this whole process, just try your best to stay calm and remind yourself that they are safe, they are loved and they will be feeding shortly.
- So, when they are both dressed and back in the bouncy seats in the nursery, play soft music and feed them their last nighttime feeding. (Don't forget to burp them.)
- Swaddle them both tightly, **if under 3 months of age,** using the Moms on Call Swaddle technique outlined at momsoncall.com
- Place them in the crib; turn on the white noise and turn off the lights.
- The babies can sleep in the same crib or separate cribs. They can even have their own room, if you have the space.

5. Having twins is a loud endeavor

Honestly, it can feel like someone is crying or fussing almost all day (and sometimes it's the momma!). We cannot hold them both every minute. They will learn how to wait, how to accommodate each other and they learn how to self-soothe earlier because it is just a part of life as a twin. YOU CAN SUCCESSFULLY RAISE THESE LITTLE ONES—JUST RESOLVE YOURSELF TO THE FACT THAT IT WILL BE LOUD AND THAT IS OK. Once they are over three months, letting them cry takes on new meaning with multiples. However, we have often found that one twin can wake and scream while the other sleeps as if nothing is happening, so do not assume that the crying child will wake the sleeping child. When you have a firm nighttime routine, even if the sleeping child awakens, they can both learn to soothe themselves to sleep if given three to five nights of consistency. I know that you do not want the 'good sleeper' to have to suffer, but his/her help is needed in teaching the other twin that screaming does not get you an automatic "get out of crib free" card.

6. Remember, it gets easier as they get older. Twins

are incredibly labor intensive for the first three years. Double the work, but double the love! The great news is that they will hit a period of time when they are continuous playmates. It is easier to have two 18 month olds, because you are not their only source of entertainment. They will play together and keep each other amused for years. It is wonderful. (Jennifer—My mom is a twin and she described it this way: "Having a twin is not like having another brother or sister, it's like having another you.")

SECTION TWO: COMMON ILLNESSES

A Quick Reference Guide To Common Illnesses For This Age Group

"The glory of the LORD shall be your rear guard."
Isaiah 58:8

COMMON ILLNESSES

"I am not sure if this fussiness is teething or an ear infection."

Here are some general descriptions of illnesses that are usually seen between 0-6 months. The following pages are for reference only. These pages are not to be used for diagnostic purposes. Only qualified medical professionals are able to accurately diagnose and treat an illness.

The illnesses that will be described in the following pages are:
Fever
Common Colds
Coughing
Falls
Lacerations
Otitis Media (Ear Infections)
Vomiting
Diarrhea
Reactive Airway Disease/Bronchitis
Infant Nasal Congestion

We also wanted to share with you a list of general symptoms that require immediate medical care. This list includes but may not be limited to:
- Rectal temperature 100.4° F or higher in a baby under 3 months of age
- Seizure activity

- Unresponsiveness
- **Inconsolable** crying for 2 or more hours
- Abdominal pain that hurts worse (baby cries) if you press one inch to the right or left of the bellybutton.
- A bright red or purple pin-prickly rash that does not blanch to white when you apply pressure with your finger. This rash is noticeable and sometimes almost looks like freckles. In a child who is lethargic and has a fever, this is one sign of meningitis.
- Hive-like rash all over with facial swelling around the lips and eyes that has a sudden onset.
- Any difficulty breathing—if you are concerned that your child is unable to get air in and out of their lungs, you should be at the ER. Difficulty breathing can be accompanied by the following symptoms:
  - Ribs becoming pronounced on inhalations.
  - Squeaky noise on exhalations.
  - Breathing faster than 60 times per minute. (Place your hand on the child's chest and count how many times the chest rises in one full minute.)
  - Coarse noise when inhaling (stridor) that sounds like a gasp or squeak with each breath.
  - Lips are blue or purple.
  - Cannot stop coughing long enough to breathe.

FEVER

"I think my baby has fever, but I am too scared to take a rectal temperature."

For a demonstration of how to properly take an infant's temperature, see momsoncall.com.

Even a mild fever in an infant **under** **3 months** of age is a reason to seek immediate medical care. This is because their immune system has not had a chance to fully develop. So, it is imperative that you are able to take an accurate temperature. When taking the baby's temperature, we recommend taking rectal temperatures exclusively until the baby is over 18 months old. That is the most accurate way to take a temperature. The ear thermometers, forehead thermometers and pacifier thermometers are just not as accurate in infants.

Interestingly, at 3 months of age, the magic immunity fairy shows up and then babies can tolerate higher temperatures. In fact, after three months of age, fever can be quite helpful. Our bodies are designed to fight off infection. One way that the body does that is to turn up the heat when a virus or bacteria is detected, hoping the bacteria or virus will not want to stick around if it gets too hot. So, mild fevers in babies **over** **3 months old** can be quite beneficial.

A normal rectal temperature is between 97-99.8 degrees Fahrenheit.

> **Note:** Each individual pediatrician can have varied guidelines on fever management. Ask your pediatrician for a "Fever Handout." This will help you to know what treatments they recommend and when they want you to call their office.

Taking a Rectal Temperature (see a demo at momsoncall.com)

1. Lubricate the thermometer with a pea-sized amount of Vaseline®.
2. Lay infant on back as if changing a diaper.
3. Lift legs so rectum is easily seen.
4. Press button on thermometer to turn it on.
5. Insert thermometer into rectum about ¼ inch or until you can no longer see the silver tip of the thermometer.
6. Hold thermometer in place 3 minutes or until it beeps (most digital thermometers only take about one minute before they beep).
7. Remove and read thermometer.

Daytime and Nighttime Treatment <u>under</u> 3 months

- o For babies under 3 months of age—call the pediatrician if the rectal temperature is 100.4° F or higher, no matter what time of day it is.
- o Do not give any fever control medications to an infant under 3 months of age without the expressed consent of your pediatrician.
- o Fevers generally subside during the day and spike in the late afternoon.
- o The only time that we would tolerate a rectal fever over 100.4° F in an infant under 3 months of age is the 24 hours after the 2-month

immunizations. Your pediatrician will guide you in the care of the baby for that time period.

Daytime treatment over 3 months

- o May treat with Acetaminophen with the approval of the pediatrician.
- o Treat the child, not the numbers on the thermometer. We are much more worried about a child that has a mild fever but is lethargic (like a wet noodle all day) than we are a child with a 104°F rectal temperature who is running around like nothing is wrong.

Nighttime Treatment over 3 months of age

- o Put child in the crib or toddler bed wearing cool cotton clothing. No fleece zip-ups or warm blankets. Temperature of the home should be between 68-72 degrees.
- o If he/she wakes up and feels very hot, undress the child down to the diaper/underwear and give whatever fever control medicine is due next, and then avoid taking their temperature for ten minutes. (The temperature will spike right when the child awakens. If we give the child about 10 minutes of being undressed, the fever will generally come down 1-2 degrees all by itself. This helps us to avoid a big parental breakdown over a 105°F rectal temp.)
- o There is normally a wait at the ER and by the time you have given a child fever control medicine and arrived at the ER, the fever is under control. However, high fevers that are accompanied by other symptoms that may need to be evaluated are, but not limited to:
  - o Neck stiffness

- Bright red or purple rash that does not blanch or lighten with pressure
- Persistent vomiting (more than twice)
- Inconsolable crying greater than one hour
- Difficulty breathing (Not increased breathing; respirations will be increased when they have a fever.)
- Seizure activity—violent shaking
- Babies over 3 months can generally take acetaminophen but babies have to be at least 6 months old to take ibuprofen products.

When to seek medical care

Under 3 months of age
- Seek immediate medical care if the rectal temperature is 100.4°F or higher.
- There is one exception to this rule, which is the 24 hours after they get the immunizations at 2 months of age. You pediatrician will give you a handout about that expected recovery period.

Over 3 months of age
- Call the pediatrician for a fever over 101.5°F rectally
- A baby with any temperature that is lethargic (like a wet noodle) all day. Any baby that is not having at least 20-30 minute periods of playfulness at any temperature can be a sign of illness.
- Fever accompanied by other symptoms such as, but not limited to: a rash, vomiting, decreased movement of a limb, difficulty breathing, inconsolable crying longer than an hour or an

abdomen that is hard like a table when the baby is at rest

> **Note:** Acetaminophen does not cure the cause of the fever. It is for comfort only. Once these medications wear off, the fever will come back until they are no longer sick. Often, the child's temperature will not come all the way back down to normal. It can hover between 101-102°F rectally in an infant over 3 months even with fever control medicines.

EYE DRAINAGE

"My 2 month old has some white-ish discharge in the corner of her eyes?"

There are many reasons that a baby can experience eye discharge. The most common is a blocked tear duct.

Blocked Tear Duct
- o Watery eyes
- o Occasional white-ish to yellow discharge (several times per day)
- o Absence of any redness or irritation to the upper or lower eyelids or sclera (white part of the eye)
- o Usually resolves on its own by 4-6 months of age

Treatment
- o Watch the "tear ducts" video demonstration at momsoncall.com.
- o Always be sure to wash your hands thoroughly before touching the baby's face.
- o Wipe the outer lids and corner of the eye with a soft, warm washcloth.
- o With your pinky or forefinger, massage the inner corner of the eye at either side of the bridge of the nose.

When to seek medical care:
- o Thick yellow or green discharge that reappears after wiping away several times a day

- Eye redness or swelling (especially swelling that goes up to the eyebrow, or below the eye approximately one inch or lower)
- Symptoms appeared immediately after a possible foreign body entered the eye.
- Frequent rubbing
- Fever—ask your pediatrician for a fever handout.
- Occurs past 6 months of age.

Other causes of eye discharge: Can be viral, allergy-related or bacterial.

Viral
Signs
- Eye redness on the inner lids and/or white part of eye (sclera)
- Watery discharge or thick mucus discharge from eyes. (Usually occurs with a cold and it can produce crustiness in the morning.)

Treatment
- Wipe away any mucus with a warm (not hot) washcloth while eyes are closed

When to seek medical care
- No improvement of symptoms in 2-3 days
- Eye redness or swelling, especially swelling that goes up to the eyebrow or below the eye approximately one inch or lower
- Fever
- Sensitivity to light

Bacterial Eye Infections

Signs
- Yellow-green discharge from eyes that has to be wiped away every 20-30 minutes
- Usually will have pinkness or redness to white part of the eye (sclera)
- Puffiness to eyelids
- It can also produce crustiness in the morning but the mucus keeps reoccurring every 20-30 minutes, even when awake.

Treatment
- Antibiotic eye drops (have to be prescribed by the pediatrician)
- Warm compresses with a clean, warm (not hot) washcloth

When to seek medical care
- No improvement in symptoms after using antibiotic drops for 2 days
- Showing signs of an ear infection (see section on ear infections.)
- Fever—ask your pediatrician for a fever handout.
- Swelling of the eyelids that goes up to the eyebrow or down to the area where we usually get dark circles under our eyes when we do not get enough sleep

Note: Always remember to wash your hands frequently.

COMMON COLDS

It is quite common for babies to have nasal congestion as long as there is no cough or fever. Babies who are in daycare, church nursery or playgroup can expect to have between 4-8 viral colds between October and February! It makes for quite the healthy immune system (so, no guilt, working mommas!).

Colds

Signs (may have some but not all of these signs)
o   Runny nose
o   Nasal congestion
o   Watery eyes

Relief measures if approved by your pediatrician:
o   Use non-medicated saline nose drops. Instill 2-3 drops in each nostril. You can use the drops 5-6 times a day. It breaks up the thicker congestion. Saline is not harmful to the eyes or mouth so if you miss that little nostril, it will be fine.
o   After you instill the non-medicated saline drops, if they still seem congested, you can use the bulb syringe to suck out the mucus. Only use the bulb syringe 3-4 times per day or it will become an irritant. Use bulb syringe to suck the saline out of the nostrils. Depress bulb, hold one nostril closed, insert tip in open nostril. At the same time, slowly remove the bulb syringe while releasing the suction of the bulb and doing a sweeping motion in nostril. Use preferably

before meals and before bed.
- Temperature in home: winter 68-70 degrees; summer 72-74 degrees
- Dress the baby as you would dress yourself, as far as layering and seasonal appropriateness. If you are wearing long pants and a long sleeve shirt, then baby should be in long baby pants and a long sleeve baby shirt. May use a short-sleeve onesie underneath.
- May use a cool mist humidifier.
- If the nose is very runny and the baby is not resting well, check with your pediatrician.
- You may clean the outer lids of eyes with a warm washcloth several times a day.
- If the child has fever, see fever section of this book.
- Increase fluids. The child may not want to eat as they often swallow a bunch of mucus down the back of their throat. This makes them lose their appetite (understandably!).
- Generally with runny noses, it bothers us more than it bothers them.

When to seek medical care
- Frequent cough with no improvement after doing above (frequent=several times/hour)
- Chest sinking in when breathing, ribs pronounced during inhalations
- Nostrils flaring
- Wheezing (whistle or squeaking sound)
- Stridor noise made on inhale when not coughing; tight sounding
- Breathing faster than 60 respirations/minute
- Call pediatrician if the rectal temperature is more than 100.4°F in a baby under 3 months of

age or 102.5°F in a baby between 3-6 months of age.

- o Symptoms last longer than 10 days.
- o Pulling on ears and/or not sleeping well for 2-3 nights
- o Worsening sore throat or copious (freakishly large amount) drooling

---

Note: Colds are not curable. Comfort measures are used to help with symptoms. No medicine approved in children will make the cold go away any faster. There are hundreds of different cold viruses, and most healthy children will get 6-10 colds/year. Careful and frequent hand washing can help manage the transmission of these viruses. We recommend keeping baby wipes in several rooms of the house and washing down everyone's hands several times a day.

COUGH

Infants often have a stuffy nose, but a frequent cough is reason to call the pediatrician.

Signs
- A productive (bringing up mucus) cough that often gets worse when activity is increased or the child is in a horizontal position.

Treatment
- Cool mist humidifier in the room at night, especially if you are running the heat in the house
- Nasal saline: 1-2 drops in each nostril as often as needed (Use the nasal syringe to suck out the mucus only about 3 times per day immediately after the saline.)
- Temperature in the home should be between 68-72 degrees

When to seek medical care
- Any frequent cough in a baby under 6 months of age is to be evaluated by their pediatrician (frequent =more than 10 times in a day or several times an hour).
- There is a history of Reactive Airway Disease or asthma, or your child ever needed an inhaler or breathing treatment in the past.
- A rectal temperature of 100.4°F in a baby under 3 months of age
- Lethargic all day (like a wet noodle)

- Any signs of difficulty breathing, such as:
    - Ribs getting pronounced on inhalations
    - Squeaky noise on exhalations
    - Breathing faster than 60 times per minute (Place your hand on the child's chest and count how many times the chest rises in one full minute.)
    - Coarse noise when inhaling (stridor) sounds like a gasp or squeak with each breath
    - Lips are blue or purple.
    - Cannot stop coughing long enough to breathe.

FALLS

Unfortunately, your baby is not going to send out a text when they are ready to roll over. We recommend always keeping babies on the lowest surface possible and when they are in the bouncy seat, swing or car seat, that they are always strapped in completely. However, even with all the safety measures in place, babies can fall.

It is common for a baby between 3 and 6 months to roll off the bed, couch or changing table. The good news is that God knew that babies would do this and He specifically designed them to tolerate minor falls. The fall is generally harder on the parent than on the baby.

Head injury with no lacerations:
- May apply ice packs to decrease swelling for 20 minutes if tolerated.
- Do not give any pain medications.
- After your child goes to sleep the first time after a head injury, make sure they can be awakened every 30 minutes for 2 hours. Keep in mind what is normal for your child.
- Check pupils to make sure they get smaller when the child is exposed to bright light. Turn lights off and check pupils with a penlight. DO NOT USE A FLASHLIGHT. They are often too bright and can damage the baby's eyes.

When to seek medical care - Watch for these symptoms for 48 hours:

- Persistent vomiting (more than twice)
- Pupils not reacting to light by getting smaller, or one pupil is large and the other small
- Marked sensitivity to light
- Difficulty awakening; seems confused
- Seizure like movement of any limb
- Breathing abnormally
- Extreme moods—either an hour of inconsolable crying or marked lethargy
- Not urinating
- Not moving a limb or sensitive when a limb is moved or touched
- Abdominal pain—the baby cries out when you touch the abdomen (make sure your hands are not too cold)
- If the fall was from a distance greater than four feet, you suspect that the baby's neck got twisted and/or the baby is not moving or crying: DO NOT MOVE THE BABY. Immediately call 911.

LACERATIONS

Clean well with soap and water. Apply pressure for as long as it takes to stop the bleeding.

When to seek medical care:
- o If wound edges are not touching or wound is gaping
- o Bleeding does not stop with pressure within 5-10 minutes
- o Bleeding is severe and/or pulsating out of the body
- o Any laceration on the face

Note: You have a right to ask for a plastic surgeon to repair any facial lacerations if you so choose. However, the best way to access a plastic surgeon is through the local ER.

OTITIS MEDIA (EAR INFECTIONS)

Ear infections/otitis media: Usually starts with a cold. The fluid that the cold produces becomes trapped behind the eardrum. Bacteria and viruses love to live in that warm, moist environment and begin to grow. Once the area has become infected with bacteria or a virus, more fluid collects behind the eardrum and causes pressure; babies generally experience discomfort.

Over 80% of ear infections are viral. That means that antibiotics will not help the ear infection to get better. Time, patience and comfort measures are the key. However, if your pediatrician prescribes antibiotics, then it is fine to administer them. The recent outbreaks of antibiotic resistant bacteria are secondary to the overuse of antibiotics so allow the doctor to help you use discretion when treating any illnesses, ear infections included. Remember, ear infections may cause discomfort, but are typically not life-threatening. (Laura has had to sit up with Blake many nights due to ear pain and pressure—no fun!)

Signs
- Ear pain—pulling at ear frequently
- Crying when laying flat
- Not sleeping well
- Fever for more than 2-3 days (although ear infections are frequently present without a fever)
- Cold symptoms

Treatment
- o OTC - May use acetaminophen for pain control if prescribed by your pediatrician
- o Cool mist humidifier in the room at night to help with the cold symptoms
- o Saline nasal spray
- o It is fine to let the sleep patterns get interrupted when your child has pain or illness. We can always be back on track in about three nights when they feel better.

When to seek medical care
- o No improvement of above symptoms within 3-4 days

Note: Ear infections can occur in babies who have no symptoms at all. This is an impossible disorder to treat based on symptoms alone. Sometimes we will find ear infections in children who are being seen for a physical exam and have no symptoms. This is a difficult area for moms. The key is to watch your child for classic symptoms. In the absence of symptoms, there is no way to know when to take your child to the pediatrician. However, if your child is only pulling at the ear but is sleeping and eating well, then it is okay to wait a day or two before making an appointment.

VOMITING

Vomiting: large amounts of vomit, with forceful emptying of stomach contents, more than 2-3 times. This is different than spitting up, not because of the forcefulness, but because of the frequency. Vomiting happens every 30-45 minutes regardless of feedings, whereas spitting up occurs at various times of day most often within 30 minutes of a feeding.

Although there are various causes of true vomiting, we see it most often associated with a gastrointestinal virus. These types of viruses usually start with vomiting every 30-45 minutes for the first 6-8 hours then maybe an isolated episode of vomiting on day two or three. Diarrhea will often accompany these symptoms and it lasts for 5-7 days. (See diarrhea section.)

Under 3 months—contact your pediatrician if experiencing persistent vomiting,

Treatment for babies over 3 months:
- o Try to wait about an hour after the child vomits.
- o Then you can try one tsp of clear liquids (water, Pedialyte or breastmilk) every 10 minutes for the first 2-3 hours while awake, with an occasional teaspoon of heavy peach syrup (not to exceed two teaspoons of peach syrup in 24 hours). Now you know why we mentioned the peaches in heavy syrup in the general shopping list! It coats the stomach and helps the baby keep the liquids down.

- You can then begin to increase the amount of clear liquids by adding another teaspoon of clear liquids every ten minutes for the next 2-3 hours. (One teaspoon, wait ten minutes, two teaspoons, wait ten minutes, three teaspoons and so on.) Sucking on popsicles or a wet washcloth is a way of ensuring that they are not swallowing too much at one time. You can sit on the couch and give sips of clear liquids from a medicine dropper if you need to as well.
- If your baby does not take a bottle then you can breastfeed for 5 minutes at each teaspoon time listed above. If the baby stays latched and they get too much at once, the baby will be fine.
- If the child goes 6-8 hours without vomiting, try to breastfeed a limited amount, increasing as tolerated or use 1-2 ounces of formula every 30 minutes for 2-3 hours as tolerated.
- If no vomiting after 12 hours, begin returning to a normal diet slowly.
- If the baby vomits during any of above, return to step one.
- Avoid giving medicines for 8 hours (with the approval of the pediatrician).

Common Errors
- Giving too much fluid at one time.
- Not waiting the hour before beginning fluids.

Sometimes when a gastrointestinal virus is causing vomiting in a child, no matter what you feed them or how often you feed them, the vomiting will continue. If your child is crying for fluids and it has not been an hour after vomiting, it is okay to give it, just try to have them drink slowly. (We realize that you only have so much control over how quickly they drink.) When they are experiencing these symptoms, it is crucial to monitor for the following additional symptoms.

When to seek medical care

Signs of dehydration

- o Not urinating at least every 6 hours (You may want to place toilet tissue in the diaper to check for wetness because the absorbent nature of today's diapers makes it hard to tell if the baby has urinated at all.)
- o When you run your pinky finger over the inside of their bottom lip, it is dry and tacky as opposed to smooth and moist.
- o Tries to cry but cannot cry tears
- o Marked lethargy
- o Unable to hold down one teaspoon of fluid after 2-3 attempts (Remember to wait 30 minutes to an hour after each vomiting episode)
- o Vomits blood
- o Neck stiffness
- o Rash
- o Vomiting that continues > 24 hours
- o Fever (see fever section)
- o Vomiting bile—fluorescent yellow or green goo
- o Abdomen hard and tender at rest (hard like a table top, as opposed to soft like a really full balloon)
- o Blood in stool (more than 1 tsp bright red blood)
- o Call pediatrician if the baby is under 3 months of age and has a rectal temperature of 100.4° F or higher or if they are over 3 months of age and have a fever of 102.5°F rectally or higher.

DIARRHEA

"My 5-month-old has had diarrhea that exploded out of the diaper 5 times today. I've had to change his clothes every time."

Diarrhea can be caused by a gastrointestinal virus and can generally last 5-7 days. However, sometimes babies may have a day of diarrhea secondary to mild stomach irritation, and this will pass in one or two days.

Signs:
- More than 5 watery stools in a 24-hour period.

Relief measures—We do not like to give medication that claims to stop diarrhea for infants or kids under 2 years old. This is because most diarrhea is caused by a gastrointestinal virus that will run its course. We want the diarrhea to get out of the baby's system. This is the body's natural way of handling this kind of virus.

Infants
- Formula fed: Continue formula feeding as usual.
- Breast-fed: Continue to breastfeed.
- Baby food for babies > 4 months old: Baby foods that are starchy are good choices, i.e., cereal, applesauce, bananas, carrots, mashed potatoes.

Note: Regardless of how you feed diarrhea, it will generally run its course. However, it's probably not the time to get Mexican for dinner.

When to seek medical care
- o 8 or more watery stools a day for 5 days.
- o Blood or mucus in stool.
- o Fever (see Fever section)
- o Abdominal tenderness/hard at rest.
- o **Any signs of dehydration:**
  - o Longer than 6 hours without urinating
  - o No tears when crying.
  - o Inside of lips feel dry when you swipe your pinky finger along the inside of bottom lip
  - o Increased lethargy

Note: Diarrhea is very contagious. All family members need to wash hands well after changing diapers and/or using the toilet.

REACTIVE AIRWAY DISEASE/ BRONCHITIS/BRONCHIOLITIS

"We went to the doctor and got diagnosed with Reactive Airway Disease. How do I know if the baby is getting any better?"

Upper respiratory viruses can trigger the airways to swell and become more narrow. These airways are lined with mucus and when they narrow, it is hard for the baby to dislodge the mucus. The medication Albuterol/Xopenex/Proventil may be prescribed and given through a nebulizer or inhaler and will help open up the airway so the child can move air through the airways and dislodge the mucus.

What to expect: In the first 24 hours of treatment, the baby will:
- Get a more frequent, more productive sounding cough. The cough will slowly improve after the first 24-48 hours and should be markedly improved within 5 days of beginning treatment.
- The baby may seem like they have a rapid heartbeat and may be on the "hyper" side for the first night or two of treatment. This is the trade-off for being able to breathe and will subside in a day or two.
- The baby may have *isolated* (i.e., not persistent like every 30-45 minutes) episodes of vomiting (mucus triggers the gag reflex).

When to seek medical care: Sometimes the airways do not respond to the medications in a way that improves breathing. The signs that the symptoms are getting worse are:

- Retractions: this is when the ribs get more pronounced when inhaling. You can almost count the ribs with each inhalation. This is an indication that the child is using accessory muscles to move the air in and out of the lungs. They are working too hard to get the air they need.
- Respirations are faster than 60 times in one full minute. Put your hand on the child's chest and count how many times the chest rises in one full minute. (If you count more than 60, recheck in 3-4 minutes; if still above 60, seek medical care.) Normally, a baby or young child will breathe 20-30 times per minute.
- Bluish or purplish hue around lips
- Shortness of breath with moderate activity
- Audible wheezing—this is a squeaky sound when exhaling as opposed to a rumbling or mucousy sound.
- Coughing so frequently that they cannot get air in between coughing fits
- Mucousy sounding breathing, with every breath that is not cleared with a cough
- Symptoms are unchanged after the first 24 hours of treatment

SECTION THREE: FEEDING

Feeding Without Fretting

"When wisdom enters your heart, and knowledge is pleasant to your soul, discretion will preserve you; understanding will keep you"
Proverbs 2:10-11

GENERAL FEEDING

At Moms on Call we believe in meeting you where you are—whether you are nursing exclusively, bottle feeding or a combination of both.

There are three options with feedings
- Breastfeeding
- Bottle feeding (using pumped breastmilk, formula or both)
- A combination of breast and bottle feeding

You can choose any of the above in any combination as it suits your family and personal beliefs.

The First Two Weeks
- Feed on demand every 2-3 hours from the <u>start</u> of one feeding to the **start** of the next.
- Feeding should not take any longer than 30-45 minutes start to finish, including burping (for both breast and bottle fed babies).
- Only spend about 2-3 minutes burping (do it ¾ of the way through the feeding and at the end).
- The most challenging part is keeping them awake: Scratch the bottoms of their feet, undress them down to the diaper or wipe their heads with a cool washcloth to help them stay awake for the feeding.
- Extend tons of grace—you are both just getting the hang of this. The first two weeks are a transition period for the whole family.

The following feeding information should be used as a general guideline. We found that this is what moms really want to know. We do not want you to feel trapped by the numbers or times indicated. This is just a helpful gauge for those moms who feel that they need some direction. To put all of the guidelines together in an easy-to-follow format, see the section entitled "Typical Days."

General Feeding Guidelines

(Babies up to 12 months need at least 24 ounces of breastmilk or formula per day)

The first two weeks
- About 7-8 feedings per day
- Feedings should take no longer than 45 minutes
- 2-3 ounces per feeding (maybe an occasional 4 ounces)

2-4 weeks
- Still 7-8 feedings per day
- Feeding should not take longer than 30 minutes.
- 3-4 ounces per feeding (maybe an occasional 5 ounces)

4-8 weeks
- 6-7 feedings per day lasting up to 20-30 minutes each
- 4-5 ounces per feeding (maybe an occasional 6 ounces)

2-4 months
- 5-7 feedings a day lasting 15-20 minutes each
- 5-6 ounces per feeding (maybe an occasional 7-8 ounces)

4-6 months
- 4-5 feedings per day lasting 12-15 minutes each (up to 20 minutes for breastfeeding babies)
- 6-8 ounces per feeding (maybe an occasional 9 ounces)
- Introduction of baby foods 1-3 times per day

BREASTFEEDING

"How do I tell if my baby is getting enough?"

Many breastfeeding moms share this common concern. We cannot measure in ounces how much breast milk a baby swallows each feeding. However, we do have some guidelines that are helpful in determining if the baby is getting the breast milk they need.

Is the baby getting enough?

- o Is satisfied after nursing.
- o Urinates at least every other feeding.
- o Gains approximately an ounce a day for the first few weeks (with the exception of week 1 when newborns commonly lose weight).
- o Inside of bottom lip is smooth and moist.
- o Soft spot is not markedly sunken.
- o Periods of alertness that last at least 20-30 minutes several times a day (after 2 weeks of age).
- o Let-down reflex is present for mom.

How often? How long?

- o The first 2 weeks, nurse on demand about every 2- 3 hours.
- o Over 2 weeks of age—every 3 hours is sufficient during the day. At night, may go longer, as much as 4-6 hours as long as the baby is healthy and

beginning to gain weight.
- See the "Typical Days" section of this resource for schedules with times!
- Nurse on the first breast, the "entrée," for up to 20 minutes or until the breast is soft and mushy. That ensures your infant is getting the high-fat, calorie-rich hind milk. Burp the baby for 2-3 minutes and then offer the second breast, as "dessert" for 5-10 minutes. Burp again for 2-3 minutes and we are done.
- Alternate which breast you start with at each feeding. (i.e. start with the left breast at 9 a.m. and the right breast at noon.)
- You can pump as soon as the baby goes down for a nap (see typical daily schedules). You can pump just the breast that was second in the feeding or pump both.
- Amount of time nursing depends on the baby's weight and age. That said, the below are simply general guidelines.
  - First two weeks: up to 45 minutes per feeding
  - 2-4 weeks of age: up to 30 minutes per feeding
  - 4-8 weeks of age: up to 25 minutes per feeding (an occasional 30 minute feeding)
  - 2-4 months of age: up to 20 minutes per feeding (an occasional 25 minute feeding)
  - 4-6 months of age: are usually able to get what they need in 15-20 minutes per feeding
- Some babies as young as 3-4 months of age can get what they need in 15 minutes, as they become more efficient feeders.
- As the breastfeeding times decrease, your

breasts will also start to remain more mushy and you experience less engorgement.

- o Your body adjusts to an increase or decrease in demand per time of day in 3-4 days. (So, if the baby stops feeding at 2 a.m. for three days in a row, your body will stop producing at 2 a.m. but you will not lose your whole supply.)
- o Healthy babies who are gaining weight can begin sleeping through the night at 8-12 weeks of age if we follow the routines and guidelines outlined in this book. We see it every day. But you can feed them in the night as long as *you* want to.

Latching:

- o Rooting reflex: Bring baby close to your breast, then stroke the baby's cheek. Your baby will turn their head and open their mouth.
- o Put as much of the areola into the baby's mouth as possible. NEVER allow the baby to suck on nipple only (it is ineffective and hurts the Mommy).
- o Holding breast from below will help put the breast into the correct position.
- o Place the baby's body directly facing the breast.
- o If not latched on correctly, remove by placing finger gently on the corner of baby's mouth to break suction. Try above steps again.

Positions

- o **Cradle Hold:** Sitting in your lap with baby's head in the crook of your arm. Baby's chest should be against your chest so that they do not have to turn their head to reach your nipple.

- **Lying Down:** Lay on your side and place the baby on their side facing you, with the baby's head at your breast.
- **Football Hold:** Hold your baby like a football along your forearm, with baby's body on your arm and their face toward your breast. Use your other hand to support the position of the baby's head.
- Find a relaxed and comfortable position. Change positions with different feedings.
- Have 4-5 pillows of different sizes. One to support your back and the others can be used creatively until you are completely comfortable and the baby is supported right beneath your breast. Which means you may have to put a rolled-up blanket or another pillow *under* the Boppy to ensure that you can feed the baby without having to hunch over or lift up the baby. (Boppy pillows or other nursing pillows are great. These saved my aching back when I was nursing my twins—Jennifer.)

Nipple Care

- After each feeding, coat nipples with some breast milk.
- Allow nipples to air dry.
- If cracked, apply 100% lanolin to nipples after feedings. (If allergic to wool, do not use lanolin).
- Make sure the infant is latching correctly.
- If sore, begin feeding on the less sore nipple.
- If the pain is severe, may need to pump until nipples heal and contact your OB/GYN.

Plugged ducts: Hard, tender lump in your breast, caused by incomplete emptying of the breast milk

- Nurse on the tender side first.
- Massage the breast with the lump, trying to express extra milk.
- Apply moist heat to breast. Shower or bathe while massaging and expressing extra milk.

Engorgement: Large firm and tender breasts. Lasts until your body gets used to making and releasing milk. Once your baby is nursing well and milk is flowing easily, there will be less swelling and firmness.

- Warm breast before nursing with warm washcloth.
- Gently massage breast while nursing.
- Cool washcloths to breast between feedings.
- Cabbage leaves: Put thoroughly washed and dried crisp, cold, green cabbage leaves over your engorged breasts. Leave on for 20-30 minutes until leaves are wilted. These are great because they fit right into your bra.
- If so engorged that it is difficult for baby to latch on, you may need to pump or hand-express some milk before feeding.

Mastitis (Breast infection): Achy, flu-like symptoms, fever, chills, headache, breast pain, breast redness, firmness.

- Call your physician immediately if you have any of these symptoms.
- Take all of the antibiotic prescribed.
- Rest and stay in bed.
- Drink plenty of fluids.
- Nurse more often, especially on the side that is infected.
- Warm washcloth to breast before feeding.

When to call your OB/GYN:

- Fever   or chills
- Headache
- Flu-like symptoms
- Pain/redness to breast
- Nipples that sting or burn
- Shooting pains in your breast during nursing
- Painful lump

Basic Instructions for those who just want to use occasional bottles

If you are planning to go back to work, are excited about seeing Dad enjoy the sweet thrill of feeding his baby or just want an occasional babysitter, then we want the baby to be familiar with feeding from a bottle. So, between 2-3 weeks of age, it is good to have at least one bottle feeding per day, at the same time each day, so the baby can get the hang of it.

Becoming familiar with the bottle

- Start around 2-3 weeks of age (Some babies have to start sooner if they are having trouble gaining weight but the pediatrician will instruct you on what to do if that is needed.)
- The bedtime feeding is our favorite one for babies who are getting familiar with the bottle.
- Bottle feed every night at the last bedtime feeding (with either breast milk or formula).
- If you would like to breastfeed at the last nighttime feeding, you can breastfeed on one side for 10-15 minutes and then "top off" with a bottle for 10 minutes.

- If you are using a bottle for the whole feeding, this is a great time to allow someone else to enjoy feeding the baby while you pump.

Breastfeeding Storage and Handling of Breast Milk

- Wash hands well.
- Store milk in plastic rather than glass.
- Label each with the date and time expressed.

Storage

- Freeze in 4 ounce increments using the breastmilk bags labeled with the date they were expressed.
- May be stored in the refrigerator for 72 hours after pumping.
- May be stored in freezer (5 degrees Fahrenheit - 15 degrees Fahrenheit) up to 3 months after pumping.
- Deep freezer (0 degrees Fahrenheit and below) may be stored up to 6 months.
- May be stored in the refrigerator for 24 hours after thawing.

Thawing

- In refrigerator until no more ice is present in the bag/bottle.
- Place the bag/bottle under running warm water or in a bowl of warm water. If you are thawing it in a bottle, make sure the nipple stays above the water line at all times.
- The 2-5 ounce plastic bottles often fit nicely into a coffee cup filled ½ way with warm water.
- Do not thaw milk at room temperature.

- o Do not allow thawed milk to sit for more than 2 hours at room temperature.
- o Do not refreeze thawed milk.

Thawed breastmilk in a bottle

- o **Use the old-fashioned nipple like that on the Gerber First Essentials. We cannot say this enough.** (We are not paid to say this, it is from working with thousands of babies—we just see what works.)
- o Allow 20-30 minutes to eat. If it takes an hour to feed a healthy infant then it is taking too long.
- o Begin with 2 ounces in the bottle. If they finish within 10-15 minutes, you can offer another ounce up to the 30-minute mark from the start of the feeding.
- o Never reuse breast milk that is left over in a bottle after one hour.
- o **Amounts** depend on the baby's weight and age. That said, the below are simply general guidelines.
  - o First two weeks: 2-3 ounces per feeding
  - o 2-4 weeks of age: 3-4 ounces per feeding (maybe an occasional 5 ounces)
  - o 4-8 weeks of age: 4-5 ounces per feeding (maybe an occasional 6 ounces)
  - o 2-4 months of age: 5-6 ounces per feeding (maybe an occasional 7 ounces)
  - o 4-6 months of age: 6-8 ounces per feeding (maybe an occasional 9 ounces)
- o **Progressing amounts**: When the baby is sucking the bottle dry for two bottle feedings in a row, increase by ½ - 1 ounce for subsequent feedings. (EXAMPLE: If the baby finishes 3

ounces for two feedings in a row, then have 3.5-4 ounces in the bottle for subsequent feedings. This ensures that the baby can eat more if they are hungry.)

WEANING

There are two ways to wean.
They are:
> Cold turkey
> One feeding at a time

With either method it is best to:
- Relax! Sometimes the first few feedings are a fight, especially if mom is the one doing the bottle feeding. They will get the hang of it.
- Feedings should take up to 30 minutes, but no longer than 30 minutes, and they should be able to get between 4-8 ounces in that time (if weaning at 2-4 weeks it may be more like 2-4 ounces).
- Use the Gerber First Essentials® bottles and nipples or a similar old-fashioned shaped nipple. (We actually like the 4mo+ flow if babies are having feeding difficulties.)
- Do not switch formulas every few days—pick one brand and type and stick with it.
- Stay on a very clear schedule. Use the schedules provided in this book (in the "Typical Days" chapter) according to the age of your baby.
- If your baby seems to "hate" the bottle, do not worry. It is simply unfamiliar. They can do this.
- It takes about 3 days of doing the same thing ***at the same time*** for them to attach to a new familiar. Do your best to stay calm and consistent.
- It is normal to grieve that last breastfeeding. Give

yourself some time to shed some tears and then choose to look forward to the upcoming feeding methods that you will continue to enjoy with your baby. All is not lost, you are still a good mom.

For more helpful information about formula and bottle feedings see the formula feeding section

Cold Turkey Method
- o Start with the morning feeding and replace each feeding with a bottle. Start with 4 ounces and the baby has 30 minutes to finish as much as they will eat, even if you have to add more.
- o Use the schedules listed in the "typical days" section of this book and at each breast/bottle feeding listed—use only the bottle.
- o The baby has 30 minutes at each time listed in the schedule to finish what they can get in that time. If they only eat 2-3 ounces then they will have another opportunity to feed at the next *scheduled* feeding time.
- o If, after 3 –5 days, they are still taking less than 24 ounces, contact your pediatrician.
- o For mom: Wear a very tight sports bra for about 3-4 days.

One Feeding at a Time Method
With this method, we switch one breastfeeding to a bottle every 3-5 days.
- o If we are trying bottles at all different times with all different people, nipples, methods, temperatures, etc., then they take longer to sort all that out.
- o Start with one midday feeding. Replace the **same**

midday feeding with a bottle for 3 days.

- Basically, at that feeding time, the baby has 30 minutes to get as much as they can get out of that bottle. Your job is to hold the bottle in position; and their job is to fight, spit and act like they hate it for 30 minutes. Then we are done, and **they do not eat again until the next *scheduled* feeding time**. This only lasts about 3-4 attempts/days, and then they get the hang of it.
- The trick is not to breastfeed until the next scheduled feeding time. If they only took ½ ounce at the attempted bottle-feeding, that is fine. They will eat at the next *scheduled* feeding time. (See the Typical Days section for schedule suggestions.) And this is the key to success.
- After 3-5 days, replace the second midday feeding with a bottle. This will go easier.
- You can stay here as long as you would like, but if you are ready to continue weaning, then after 3-5 days you can drop the next breastfeeding by replacing that breastfeeding with a bottle each day and repeating the above process.
- If after working on it for 3 days, you are not seeing any improvement, contact your pediatrician.

Note: Babies should be getting 24-32 ounces of formula or breast milk in a bottle per day.

FORMULA FEEDING

When choosing a formula, it is important to stick with the same brand and type of formula for at least 5 days. A baby's digestive system takes 5-7 days to adjust to the enzymes and sugars when going from breast milk to formula, or even changing from one brand of formula to another. Expect 5-7 days of fussiness, gassiness and changes in bowel habits.

Brand names of formulas:
- o   Ross products: Similac, Similac Advanced
- o   Mead-Johnson Products: Enfamil, Enfamil Lipil
- o   Store-Brands: Walmart, Target, etc.

Note: Formula companies are regulated and formulas are designed to meet the nutritional needs of your infant.

Forms of Formulas:
Powder
- o   Least expensive
- o   May be prepared ahead of time
- o   Use warm tap water to mix formula.
- o   Always add the water first so you do not make it too concentrated.
- o   Using tap water ensures the baby is getting some fluoride. In some counties boiling tap water is necessary. If you are on well water, boil your tap water for 5 minutes and then let cool.

Concentrated: Use equal amounts of tap water and formula. This mixture of formula may also be stored in the refrigerator for up to 48 hours.

Ready to feed: Most expensive. May use occasionally, but remember that ready to feed formulas do not contain any fluoride.

> **Note: When using formula, always follow the directions on the can.**

How long?
- The "Typical Days" section of this resource has progressing schedules with times and amounts!
- Typically bottle feedings take 15-20 minutes however, there are guidelines below to ensure that the feeding is not taking too long and interfering with proper digestion
- **The first two weeks** – feedings should take no longer than 45 minutes (about 7-8 feedings per day)
- **2-4 weeks**–(still 7-8 feeding per day) feeding should not take longer than 30 minutes. If feedings are taking longer than 30 minutes after the first 2-3 weeks . . .
  - Check nipples—may need to progress to the next flow level.
  - Check bottles: Make sure that you are using a nipple shaped similar to the Gerber First Essentials Bottle system, but you can experiment with other brands if needed.
  - Decrease the amount of time spent

burping the baby.
- o After doing the above, if the baby is still taking over 30 minutes, then contact your pediatrician.
- o **4-8 weeks:** 6-7 feedings per day lasting 20-30 minutes each
- o **2-4 months**: 5-6 feedings a day lasting 15-20 minutes each
- o **4-6 months**: 4-5 feedings per day lasting 12-15 minutes each

Amounts

- o Babies need between 24-32 ounces per day for the first year of life. (The first two weeks of life the baby may take less as they figure out how to feed.)
- o Begin with 2 ounces at a time. If they finish that then add an ounce more. But stick to the time limit on each feeding so their GI system can begin to get in a good solid routine. So, if they take 2 ounces in 20 minutes, you have 10 more minutes to see if they will take another ½ - 1 ounce. Do not force it.
- o Amounts depend on the baby's weight and age. That said, the below are simply general guidelines.
   - o First two weeks: 2-3 ounces per feeding
   - o 2-4 weeks: 3-4 ounces per feeding (maybe an occasional 5 ounces)
   - o 4-8 weeks: 4-5 ounces per feeding (maybe an occasional 6 ounces)
   - o 2-4 months: 5-7 ounces per feeding (maybe an occasional 8 ounces)
   - o 4-6 months: 6-8 ounces per feeding (maybe an occasional 9 ounces)

o The amount of formula can vary from feeding to feeding and day-to-day. Some days they need more and some less, just like us.

Position

o Make sure that you are both comfortable.
o Support your arm with a pillow.
o Hold the baby in a semi-upright position.
o Tilt the bottle so that the nipple and the neck of the bottle are always filled with formula.

Changing formulas:

o Do not change formulas without checking with your doctor.
o If formula is changed:
   o It will take the child several days to adjust to a new formula.
   o Stools will change and may increase or decrease and can vary from firm to loose.
   o Increased gassiness/fussiness.

Temperature for feedings: You may try different temperatures (from cool to warm) to find which your infant prefers. If warming, place bottle in a cup of warm water and ALWAYS CHECK TEMPERATURE BEFORE FEEDING. NEVER USE A MICROWAVE TO WARM BOTTLES. Microwaves heat unevenly and what you test on your wrist may feel fine, but portions of formula in the bottle can be scalding!

Gas in formula fed infants

o You may try different bottle types but the one that works the best in the thousands of households that we have been to is the old-fashioned shaped nipple like the Gerber First Essentials. (More expensive and 'breast-shaped' does not mean better quality, just better advertising.)

- o Do not burp too often. Burp once about ¾ of the way through the feeding if the baby gets squirmy and wiggly and then again at the end of the feeding.
- o You may use infant gas drops according to the package directions.

SPITTING UP

"I think my baby has reflux."

Occasionally babies will vomit or spit up after a feeding. All babies have some form of reflux. The muscle that opens and closes at the end of the esophagus does not fully mature until four months of age.

There are two types of babies that spit up, the happy ones and the unhappy ones. The unhappy ones generally get medication to help decrease the acidity of the stomach contents. That way, when the stomach contents come up the esophagus, it is much less likely to cause any discomfort.

Some babies spit up more than others. It is more related to physics than behavior. Spitting up usually resolves by 7 months of age, although babies may have a resurgence of spitting up when they learn to sit up because there is more pressure on the abdomen as those muscles are developing. The babies start to develop these great tummy muscles around 4-6 months of age while mom is still looking for a good girdle for her own tummy!

Treatment
- Keep feedings at least 3 hours apart so the tummy has time to digest, rest and reset.
- Allow the baby long stretches of sleep at night so we are not on the 24-hour digestion train—that will help to decrease the amount of time the tummy is stimulated to make more acid.

- Do not burp too often. The initial suck is the one that produces the most gas. Burping 3-4 times a feeding means 3-4 initial sucks that produce more gas.
- Burp ¾ of the way in to the feeding or, if breastfeeding, when you switch breasts and then once again at the end.
- Breastfeeding moms, make sure to empty one breast before switching to the other side.
- Do not spend more than 3 minutes trying to get a good burp.
- When burping, reposition the baby several times.
- If you are bottle-feeding, switch to Gerber First Essentials® or similar old fashioned looking nipples.

When to seek medical care:
- Persistent vomiting (every 30-45 minutes regardless of feedings)
- More than a handful, more than 3-4 times per day
- Vomiting progressively getting worse with each feeding
- Baby's stomach clenches tightly minutes after starting a feeding
- Fussy with feeding during AND after feedings
- Decrease in wet diapers—we like to see *at least* five wet diapers in 24 hours.

STARTING BABY FOODS AND SOLIDS

"When can I start baby foods? I need to know how much to feed my baby and how often to feed her."

Basics for beginners 4-6 months
You may begin baby food (stage one) between 4-5 months of age. We like to start at 4 months of age but we really want these babies to have started baby food by 5 months at the latest so that we do not miss the perfect developmental window. Be prepared to wear a good deal of baby food over the next month.

For a super easy printable feeding guide, see "The Moms on Call Baby Food Introduction Schedule" free download at momsoncall.com.

The most important thing is to have a low-stress, happy atmosphere even if the baby seems to not like it at first.

- o HAVE FUN, giggle often and take lots of pictures. We are simply getting them used to different tastes and textures.
- o RELAX, we want your face to indicate that this is normal and fun. They are watching you.
- o Babies get 100% of their nutritional needs met through the formula and breast milk until 12 months of age, so we do not need to worry about amounts.

- Sit the baby in a bouncy seat on the floor, this will be the easiest way to start feedings at this age.
- Mix 1-2 tablespoons of baby cereal with formula or breast milk until the consistency is almost like smooth yogurt.
- Use the long handled spoons and place the food on the tip of the spoon. Place the spoon in the baby's mouth and allow the spoon to sit in the baby's mouth while you hold the spoon.
- Always start new foods in the morning to see if it agrees with them.
- Order of introduction: Baby cereal first, then fruits and veggies. (See "The Moms on Call Baby Food Introduction Schedule" free download at momsoncall.com)
- If it seems to upset them (increasing fussiness and frequent spitting up), stop *that* food and wait 1-2 weeks to try that food again.
- Do not feed them out of the baby food jar; pour the food into another container and feed from there. The bacteria from their mouths (by way of the spoon) will contaminate the jar of food. Once opened, an uncontaminated jar should be refrigerated and used within 48 hours.
- Amounts are relative at this stage. The baby may take 1-2 spoons one day and 5-6 the next.
- REMEMBER, this is a gradual process however not **too** gradual. Move from a thin, yogurt-consistency to thicker consistency

with some texture (a consistency like adult rice pudding) within a little over a month.

- o Stage one: very pureed for 2 weeks
- o Stage two: thicker pureed for 2-4 weeks
- o Stage three: thickest puree until they start mushable finger foods by 7 months

- o See the section entitled "Typical Days" for a sample day with food amounts and times.
- o **Vitamins/Supplements**
  Consult your physician at the baby's next check-up to guide you in vitamin supplementation. Herbs and homeopathic remedies are usually not tested on infants and children under 6 years old. Therefore we cannot recommend any herbal preparation. That is not to say that they are harmful. There is just not enough information available about their safety when used in children or infants.

FOOD ALLERGIES

We start baby foods at 4 months of age. It is uncommon for babies to have severe allergic reactions to baby foods, however foods can cause some mild stomach upset, gas and a change in bowel habits as their little GI systems get used to the new offerings.

Common reactions: If you notice the following symptoms, monitor closely, call the pediatrician and avoid suspect food for at least 2 weeks.
- Mild splotchy pink areas on face only
- Diarrhea and/or vomiting
- Itchy skin areas, exacerbates eczema

Severe reactions: If you notice the following symptoms, call **911!**
- Sudden difficulty breathing and/or swallowing
- Wheezing
- Tightness in chest or throat
- Excessive drooling
- Facial swelling
- Hive-like splotchy rash all over (together with any of the above symptoms)

Always keep Diphenhydramine (Benadryl) on hand. May need to see an allergist if food allergies are suspected.

BABY FOOD INTRODUCTION SCHEDULE

Days 1-3
- o Begin with 1-2 tablespoons of baby cereal mixed with formula or breast milk until it is the consistency of yogurt. Give this in the morning and afternoon for three days.

Days 4-6
- o Now we add pears to the morning feeding. We can either mix it in with the baby cereal or we can give it separately.
- o Baby cereal WITH pears in the afternoon
- o We are gradually increasing the menu.

Days 7-9
- o Now we have the option of moving to three meals a day. (If you have multiple children and all you can do is two baby food feedings a day; that is fine.)
- o We can add squash to the morning feeding. We can mix the squash with baby cereal.
- o The midday feeding and/or the supper feeding is cereal, pears and squash (not necessarily mixed together).
- o A typical day can look like this:
  - o Baby cereal and pears or squash for breakfast
  - o Cereal, pears and squash for lunch
  - o Pears and squash for supper for three days

Days 10-12
- o Now we add apples to the morning feeding. We can mix it with the baby cereal or give separately.
- o Then the rest of day we have the option to give pears & squash or apples & squash (not necessarily mixed together).
- o From here it can be 3 meals a day, introducing a new food every three days and adding them to the above menu. Go back and forth between fruit and vegetables. We are looking for variety. Fruit will always taste better than vegetables no matter what order they come in.

Sippy Cups

You may begin putting small amounts of **formula/breast milk** in a sippy cup around 4-6 months of age. The baby/babies may only sip occasionally and it will take time for them to learn how to suck out of this type of cup.

- o Place the tip of the sippy cup on the tongue and hold it there for a few minutes (or as long as reality allows).
- o You may offer the sippy cup frequently, even if they only want to play with it at first. It is important to get babies used to the *presence* of the sippy cup at meals even if they do not drink from it for several months.
- o Starting the sippy cup with formula or breast milk in it will increase the chances that the baby will want to take it.
- o 2 ounces of formula or breast milk in the sippy cup at a time is fine.

o   Do not worry if they are not taking much in the sippy cup. They are just getting used to it at this time.

Formula/ Breast milk amounts:

Daily amounts
24-32 ounces/day. Once you begin baby foods and solids, you may notice a decrease in the amount of overall formula or breast milk, bringing the total closer to but not below 24 ounces/day. If nursing exclusively, they may decrease time on the breast.

SECTION FOUR: SLEEP

Establishing Healthy Sleep Habits

"If you lie down, you will not be afraid; when you lie down, your sleep will be sweet."
Proverbs 3:24

BASIC SLEEP PRINCIPLES

"How do I get my baby to sleep? Does everyone have this all worked out but me? I am so exhausted I almost fell asleep on the way to the pediatrician's office."

As long as this baby is healthy, the following advice—IF FOLLOWED—will produce a much better night's sleep. **These principles are designed to work together and if you change one or leave one out you will not get the expected results.**

We are working with the body's natural rhythm and routines to establish healthy sleep habits that benefit the entire family. Getting proper rest is essential for normal growth and development, supports the body's immune system, allows the gastrointestinal tract to function properly and is the cornerstone of healthy, happy households. In short, this is just normal.

Before we get started
- o We only do sleep training with healthy babies who are gaining weight.
- o The following principles are especially helpful for babies suffering from GI reflux
- o Sometimes we take three steps forward and one step back—this is normal as the routines are settling in. We want to avoid the knee-jerk reaction of changing everything over one bad night. Our job is to stay consistent and realistic.

Basic Moms on Call Principles

Sleep environment

o Cribs are the only sleep environment that we recommend, one less than 5 years old with a new mattress, mattress cover and tight-fitted crib sheet.

o The baby sleeps in a safe crib in their room. They rest better when they are out of the "kitchen of their favorite restaurant" (that's you!). They can smell you from a room's length away.

o The crib must be free of any stimulation such as mobiles, toys of any variety, stuffed animals, loose blankets or light up fish tanks. We like two items in the crib: (1) The baby; (2) Optional thin, mesh, breathable bumper pad secured around the perimeter to keep the arms and legs from getting stuck in between the crib slats.

o In short, the sleep environment is completely safe and so boring there is nothing to do there but sleep. We want them to associate the crib with sleep, not play.

o White noise is on all night long and must be loud enough for you to be able to hear clearly from the other side of a closed door. This helps their brains get into the deep, refreshing, REM sleep and stay there longer. Place it approximately two feet from the head of the crib, level with the mattress but not in the crib.

o White noise is only white noise, not lullabies or ocean waves. See our website for the one we like best at momsoncall.com

o At night, the room is pitch-black dark, no night-lights, closet lights or hallway lights. Blackout curtains are wonderful. However, there can be some indirect light coming through the windows for naptimes.

○ Temperature of the room is 68-72 degrees.

○ If **under** 3 months, the baby is wearing either a onesie or a light cotton sleeper and is secured in a Moms on Call swaddle.

○ If **over** 3 months, the baby is wearing a short-sleeve onesie and a light cotton sleeper, as the swaddle is no longer required at this age.

How Daytime Affects Nighttime Sleep

○ Babies learn by association and routine. Babies will associate swaddle with sleep time, crib with sleep time and white noise with sleep time. We are using the way that they learn in order to help them to learn when to sleep.

○ Keep three hours between supper and bedtime feedings. Follow the schedules listed in the "Typical Days" section of this book. It will keep enough time between supper and bedtime feedings to make sure that they are hungry enough to eat well at the bedtime feeding; which helps to sustain them through that first long stretch of sleep in the night.

○ Do not allow any naps to last longer than 2 hours. (2 ½ hours is ok for the first 4 weeks.)

○ See the "Naptime section" for more details about developing healthy naptime habits.

○ Follow the same evening routine each night. Babies have a little internal 24-hour clock and love a predictable schedule. It is how they understand the world around them.

Bedtime Routine

- The bedtime routine always begins with bath time. They have a bath every night. Water is warm. (See a demonstration at momsoncall.com)
- After the bath, and once the baby is diapered and clothed, we have what we call **"Tender Time."** Dim the lights, read a book, play soft music, sing to your baby. This is the sweetest time of day.
- Feed very well, preferably in their room, so the stimulation level is low as they get ready for nighttime sleep. Burp the baby.
- **Swaddle a baby under 3 months of age according to the Moms on Call guidelines. The arms must be securely down by their sides.**
- Turn on white noise—loud.
- You can rock the baby for a *few* minutes but place them in the crib slightly but pleasantly awake.
- When placed in the crib, after the bedtime feeding, (swaddled correctly for babies under 3 months of age), sound machine going, we can allow these little ones to settle themselves down if needed. Every 3-5 minutes you can rub, shush, jiggle and use the paci if needed until they are fast asleep. Try increasing that time each night within your comfort zone.
- No bottles in the crib, but a paci is fine.
- Make sure the room is dark. You may turn on minimal lighting when you go into the room to check on the baby so you do not trip.
- Keep the door closed.

SLEEP: 2 WEEKS-3 MONTHS

In review, the bedtime routine is as follows:
- o Warm bath
- o Tender time
- o Last nighttime feeding
- o Swaddle them right -tight, tight, tight!*
- o In the crib
- o White noise on
- o Lights out
- o Door closed

*The magic is in the correct swaddle technique. It keeps the baby safe and makes the rest of these principles work wonders! Use only the large 44x44 inch **flannel** swaddle blanket and watch how to do it at momsoncall.com. (Seriously—do it!)

Middle of the Night Feeding: 2 weeks to 3 months
When we feed a baby in the middle of the night, our goal is to keep it simple and boring.
- o Turn off the white noise for the feeding.
- o Unswaddle them.
- o Feed them for no longer than 20-30 minutes in their room.
- o Then change their diaper.
- o Swaddle them back up.
- o They can have another few sucks on the breast or bottle (maximum of 3-5 minutes).
- o Put them in the crib.
- o White noise back on.
- o Lights off.
- o Close the door.

If they are taking longer than 15 minutes to get back to sleep, then you can keep them swaddled the following night for the middle of the night feeding.

Stretching out feeding times in the middle of the night : 2 weeks – 3 months

In order to reach the goals listed in the "Typical Days" schedule, here is how we can stretch the baby longer between feedings:

> If they cry for 5 minutes in a row
>> Check the swaddle
>> Shush and rub their belly
>> Shush and gently jiggle
>> Paci
> If they cry for another 5 min. in a row
>> Check the swaddle
>> Shush and rub their belly
>> Shush and gently jiggle
>> Paci
> If they cry for another 5 min. in a row
>> Check the swaddle
>> Shush and rub their belly
>> Shush and gently jiggle
>> **Feed**

- o These 5-minute increments do NOT need to be back-to-back, for example: they could occur at 1 a.m., 1:15.a.m. and 1:30 a.m.
- o During this process, if the swaddle has loosened or an arm has gotten out, then re-swaddle even if you have to take the baby out of the crib to do so.
- o You can increase the crying time outlined above, within your comfort level, as the baby gets older.

We will always come from a position of encouragement and support. We will not judge or tear down any parent who does not choose our method. There are differing ways of raising children and if you choose another method, that is perfectly fine. We want you to be confident in how you have chosen to raise your family and live your lives—day and night—on purpose.

Swaddle essentials for babies under 3 months of age

Swaddling a baby **under 3 months of age** is like a miracle sleep trick, but they will only respond to it if it is done **_exactly_** correct and is tight in the right places.

There are many things that we have discovered about the swaddle. In order to achieve a tight, effective swaddle, the blanket has to be large and square. The blankets that are sold at popular retail stores are too small! That is why we developed and manufacture our own 44 x 44 inch large flannel wonders! It is the only way to achieve a tight, safe and effective swaddle that will make the difference between 2-3 hours of sleep in a row and 6-10 hours of sleep in a row!

You can purchase a swaddle blanket at momsoncall.com or you can make your own using light flannel fabric cut at 44x44 inches and surging the edges. Every centimeter counts when we are talking about an effective swaddle!

The second thing that you need in order to achieve a tight swaddle is an effective technique with a demonstration. Watch how to do it correctly at momsoncall.com.

It has to be exactly right and tight, tight, tight (in all the right places). These principles do not work with any other swaddle. We would love it if they did, we want this to be as easy and accessible as possible, but we literally tried every other one out there and could not get the same result.

The primary benefit of the tight swaddle is to reduce the baby's startle reflex and imitate the snug environment of the womb. Healthy babies are born with a startle reflex. This is an involuntary reaction, which causes movement in the arms that they cannot control.

Many parents will say: "He likes to have his hands up by his face, so I do not swaddle the arms." However, babies under 3 months old do not have purposeful movement of their limbs. They cannot keep their hands up by their face in the same way that they cannot hold their own bottle. If their hands are up by their face, the startle reflex will be triggered and wake them up. Swaddling them with their arms by their sides prevents the startle reflex from waking them and helps them to sleep better.

The baby may not seem as if they like the swaddle at first. They just need the opportunity to get used to it. Once they do, they will begin to associate swaddle with sleep and sometimes drift off before you can finish tucking in the last piece of material. It has always amazed us at Moms on Call, that when we get these babies swaddled *correctly*, they drift off to sleep— every baby, every time.

Swaddle Troubleshooting:

o   We do not recommend swaddling a baby at night over 12 weeks of age (naptime swaddle up to 14 weeks of age).

o   Watch the video several times and swaddle (and re-swaddle) until you feel like you have it right. It is impossible to perform the correct, tight swaddle without watching the demonstration.

o   You can use a stuffed animal in the place of the baby at first so it is not as nerve-racking!

o   When you spread the blanket on the bed and fold over the first corner (before you put the baby on top of the blanket), make sure that corner is folded over so the tip is almost parallel to the adjacent corners.

o   Make sure the arms are straight and slightly under their bottom with the baby's palms against the bed not against their own bottom.

o   Remember to pull the slack out of the blanket with each fold.

o   Begin making the "pocket" when you fold the last corner over the baby's chest and around the back.

o   Make sure that your last corner that tucks into the "pocket" is slightly wadded and not completely flat. This will help the swaddle to remain secure.

o   When you wrap the final corner around the baby—the "belt"—wrap that piece of material around the level of the baby's elbows, not the shoulders.

o   These guidelines should help you to produce that tight swaddle that helps babies to feel secure and sleep better. If the baby is routinely able to wiggle out of the swaddle, then it is time to read the "dropping the swaddle" section of this book.

SLEEP: 3-6 MONTHS (including dropping the swaddle)

If you have not enjoyed a full night's sleep prior to 3 months of age and 12 pounds, then we have great news! It is time for 10-12 hours of sleep in a row—which will support normal growth and development, support the body's immune system, allow the gastrointestinal tract to rest and is the cornerstone of healthy, happy households.

Around 3 months of age and 12 pounds, the baby is developmentally ready to find their own comfy spot. It is also time to remove the swaddle. We will remove the **nighttime** swaddle either when the child is regularly breaking out of it or they reach 12 weeks of age. The **naptime** swaddle can remain until 14 weeks of age.

Each transition takes a baby 3 nights of adjustment. So, if we make all of the ideal adjustments at one time, then we only have 3 days of adjustment instead of 3 days for each change. So, overall it is easier on the baby to settle into the ideal routine all at once. We are working with the body's natural rhythm and routines to establish healthy sleep habits that benefit the entire family.

In short, we will be:
- o Removing the swaddle.
- o Getting off the 24 hour digestion train (no more middle of the night feedings).
- o Discontinuing any middle-of-the-night paci-pong (that's what we call it when the paci

slips out, you go in, it slips out, you go in, etc.)

Prior to starting
- Review the Basic Moms on Call Principles. Remember, the crib is free of any loose objects, toys, blankets or mobiles.
- We only do sleep training with healthy babies who are gaining weight.

How daytime affects nighttime sleep
- No naps last longer than 2 hours.
- Keep at least 3 hours between supper and bedtime feedings.
- NO cluster feeding in the evening.
- Early evening is their fussy time—they have a certain amount of energy that they have to release before they are ready for bedtime.

Bedtime routine
- Warm bath
- Tender time
- Last nighttime feeding
- In the crib
- White noise on
- Lights out
- Door closed

Middle of the night 3-6 months

- IF SWADDLED, we start by taking away the nighttime swaddle first. (They can keep it at naptime until 14 weeks of age.)
- Temperature of the house is between 68-72 degrees F.
    - 68-72 degrees F: Baby is wearing a cotton, short sleeve onesie without any embroidered elements that are scratchy on the inside. Over that, the baby can wear a light, cotton, long-sleeve, long pant sleeper with footies.
- If you do not have control over the temperature in the room.
    - Cold -64-68 degrees F: Baby can wear a *fleece*, zip-up sleeper with footies.
    - Hot 73-78 degrees F: Baby is wearing short sleeve light cotton sleeper or just a onesie.
- When it is time to put the baby in the crib, they go in the crib without the swaddle and they may not be very happy about that. They will get used to it, it will just take 2-3 nights. But they can do it!
- They will spend the first night crying on and off for what may seem like much of the night. This is just part of that learning curve, they are figuring out how to find that comfy spot and they will do it, but it will take them about three nights. The frustration is actually helpful to them as they navigate that crib.
- Your job is to stay out of their way until morning. You lay them down in the crib after the last nighttime feeding and stay out until 7 a.m. That is your whole job. You provide the safe and consistent learning environment; they figure out how to move about in the crib. It is new to them

but they can do it!!

- Remember, this process can take up to three nights and in that time this child will learn how to sleep in his/her own crib.
- It is also time to get off the 24-hour digestion train. Their GI system needs a nice, long rest. So we will drop any lingering, middle of the night feedings. They will not starve. They will get what they need incrementally during the day. So if you are breastfeeding, increase the feeding time by 5-10 minutes each daytime feeding and if you are bottle-feeding, offer 1-2 more ounces per daytime feeding in the bottle. (If you are concerned about your baby's growth and development, that should be managed with the help of your pediatrician.)
- This is harder for us than it is for them, although it may not sound like it at first!
- At this age, it usually only takes about 3-4 days as long as we stay out of the way.
- THIS IS CRUCIAL! The next morning, we start the day at the same time each day, even if we have to wake them up.
- Have support. If mom and dad are living in the same home, make sure that you are both in agreement and can support each other. This will help immensely. Men are usually better at this. Help each other.
- Be consistent. If you plan to do this, commit to do it for three to five whole nights, sometimes they catch on even quicker.
- Speak the truth to your heart—**They are safe, they are loved and they can learn to do this.**
- Parents are always so afraid the child will feel abandoned. So we have to ask: Are they

abandoned? No! No, they are not abandoned. Now we are free to parent according to that simple truth. They are not abandoned and you will show up every morning at that predictable time and they will be ready for your warm embrace.

- o Somewhere between nights 7 and 10, we will have a bad night as the new routine is settling in. This is normal and does not require intervention.
- o Use this routine and do not leave out one step! This has worked for thousands of frustrated families and we are confident that it will be just as effective for you and yours.

Morning for 3-6 months

- o Starting the day on time is an important aspect of maintaining healthy sleep habits. We do not let them make up for lost sleep. We transfer lost sleep to the next scheduled sleep time.
- o Getting to sleep earlier at night (within reason) will help them to sleep later according to the times outlined in the "Typical Days" section of the book.
- o At 4 months of age we should be getting the baby in the crib by 7:30 p.m. (8 p.m. at the latest). This will help them to make it to 7 a.m. (We know that seems counterintuitive but it works!)

A few more tips for 3-6 months

Are you afraid they will wake up a sibling? We never "save" the quiet one. Siblings have an innate ability to sleep through loudness. But if another child wakes, they can get themselves back to sleep without our help and will do so better without us in the room offering up extra stimulation in the middle of the night.
We just let them work it out. First they learn how to accommodate their siblings, then they learn how to accommodate classmates, then others in the community and so on. It is a natural part of life.

Night one can be trying. You will want to run back in there and swaddle them back up. But that is counterproductive. If you want them to learn to sleep all night, without the swaddle and without a feeding, then stay out of their room, go to bed and open the door when the sun comes up just like you said. They will be ready for your loving embrace in the morning.

The morning is important, stay on schedule.
Start the day on time. We do not want them to make up for lost sleep, we want them to transfer that lost sleep to the next naptime or nighttime. Also, do not let those naps last longer than 2 hours.

Our confidence will be contagious.
This method is intent on encouraging you to support your baby as they adjust to healthy nighttime habits that will help them to be physically healthy, and equip them to enjoy life. They need long stretches of sleep just like we do. Two or three nights of hard work and you can look forward to evening and night times all the way into toddlerhood!

If we go in and some of us might, then it takes longer but it can still be done. There is not a point of no return. Regroup, reread the sleep section of the book and start fresh the next night. You can do it!!

During this 3-5 night transition, babies cry because this is not what happened yesterday and they are creatures of habit. The only way to reset that little internal clock and teach them the new schedule is to stay consistent for the amount of time it takes for them to learn (typically 3-5 nights). They will begin to learn on night 2 that you show up every morning (therefore, not feeling abandoned) and by night 3 they are really beginning to understand the new routine. By night 4 or 5, they too are enjoying the nice long stretches of sleep that allow their bodies to relax, repair and rejuvenate.

SLEEP-TIME TROUBLESHOOTING

The consistency of nighttime is such a huge piece of the puzzle and we have that in place.

Now it is a matter of working through a few details. We will get there.

1. **Missed one of the details of the nighttime plan outlined in the sleep section**. Leaving out one piece of the puzzle can affect the success of nighttime. If you did not like the white noise or fed too often in the evening, we can have wake up times in the night. Review all of the sleep guidelines and make sure that you are following each one.

2. **They are still working on increasing their intake during the day**. To ensure that the baby is getting at least 24 ounces per day, offer the baby a bottle supplement with formula or breast milk for the first and last feedings of the day x 3-4 days. If they are taking over an ounce in the supplement, then they need to have additional ounces after those feedings more regularly.

3 **The white noise machines are an essential piece of the puzzle.** Be sure to get one intended for adults so they do not have all those annoying lights. They need to be loud enough for you to hear them from outside the baby's room with the door closed.

4. Some babies over 3 months of age have a loud twilight sleep stage in the night. If they are having on and off fussiness in the night past night 5, this is typically the culprit and it is not something we can change. They are asleep and you can see on the baby monitor that their eyes are closed. They are just making some loud noise in their sleep. Occasionally the loudness of their own voice fully wakes them up. The key is that they learn how to get themselves back to sleep. This is an important and valuable life skill.

If you are having trouble beyond a week and would like to partner with a Moms on Call trained consultant, we have many options. Look us up at momsoncall.com.

So how do you handle resentful friends or neighbors when they find out that your child/children sleep all night?

At Moms on Call we are always supportive. Whatever methods that any parent chooses to put into practice is their choice. We often will say things like:

"If you need to borrow the book, I have it. But if what you are doing is working for you, then that is really great."

MAINTAINING GOOD SLEEP HABITS

"We are at my mom's for vacation and Sterling does not want to sleep. She usually goes to sleep so well."

Your child's sleep pattern may be interrupted when:

- They reach certain developmental milestones— i.e., rolling over, crawling.
- They change environments or daily routines (vacation, holidays).
- They are recovering from an illness.
- The trick is to get right back into the healthy routine as soon as possible. It is much easier to *re-establish* great sleep habits. But the longer we put it off, the longer it may take to return to the nice long stretches of sleep.
- Review the basic sleep principles outlined in the sleep sections of this book and in 1-3 nights, you will be right back on track. This is all a part of *maintaining* healthy sleep habits.
- If you go on vacation and are sharing a room or just have to keep the peace, no matter what; then return to your great sleep routines as soon as you get home.
- If your child is suffering from a virus or infection, then it is fine to go in their room at night. Provide whatever comforts they need and when they feel better, spend the 1-3 nights it will take to get them back on the great sleep routine they enjoyed prior to their illness.

NAPTIME

Naptimes – General

o   Try to get *at least* 2 naps in the crib per day (the younger they are, the more naps they need to take in a crib) as much as reality allows.

o   Allow a little bit of sunlight into the room to help regulate that natural distinction between daytime and nighttime sleep.

o   The goal of naptime is to keep them in the crib until as close to the next *scheduled* feeding time as possible (around 4-5 months, they can have some low-key awake time prior to a feeding).

o   **Under** 3 months of age, swaddle them for every naptime that they are in the crib.

o   Never share a sleep surface with an infant, it is entirely too dangerous. That means you can hold the baby at an occasional naptime as long as you are awake and alert. If you are sleepy, put the baby in the crib.

o   White noise is on LOUD and is only white noise, not lullabies or ocean waves. Use white noise for the entire naptime. See the website for the one we like best at momsoncall.com.

o   Provide a consistent nap schedule where the naps start at the same time each day. (See the "Typical Days" section of this book.)

o   Your job is to provide the routine and environment and their job is to sleep.

o   Put the child in the crib while awake.

The first two weeks
- o Babies will sleep what seems like all day long. Keep naptimes under 2½ hours between each feeding during the day. (Easier said than done—do your best.)

2-4 weeks
- o Keep naptimes to 1½ -2½ hours between each feeding with one catnap of an hour to an hour and a half after 6 p.m. (See "Typical Days.")

4-8 weeks
- o Naptimes shorten as they have more awake time after feedings.
- o Naps are 1½ – 2 hours with a 45 minute-1 hour catnap in the evening.

8-12 weeks
- o They are taking 2-3 good naps that last 1½-2 hours (typically earlier in the day) and then 1-2 catnaps (30-45 minutes) typically later in the day.
- o The evening nap becomes more unpredictable; some days they will take it and others they will not.
- o Try letting them take the last catnap in the swing (strapped in with adult supervision)
- o You may notice that they "wake up" about 30-45 minutes into every nap, this is normal. It is called "twilight sleep." They can get up at that time for two naps a day and the other two—they will fuss on and off for 15-20 minutes and then get back to sleep. You can use the paci or soothe them every 5-10 minutes as needed.

12-16 weeks
- o When they are breaking out of the swaddle

regularly, we remove it at nighttime first- see '"*Sleep 3-6 months*"

- o Once they are sleeping well at nighttime without the swaddle, we can remove it from the naps (by 14 weeks at the latest).
- o Be warned, the naps will get shorter at this point by about 15 minutes each.
- o Those first few days without the swaddle are a challenge but they can do it! They just need time and opportunity.
- o Keep them in the crib for an hour and fifteen minutes minimum for the same two naps a day that start at the same predictable times. (See "Typical Days.")
- o The morning nap is still the best one of the day. The afternoon can be good or bad and the other two naps are simply catnaps.
- o Stay consistent and they will settle into a good routine

4-6 months

- o They take a good morning nap of 1- 1½ hours.
- o Then an afternoon nap of 1 ½ - 2 hours.
- o Then a 30-45 minute catnap in the evening as needed and depending on how the day is going.
- o Keep the white noise on loud and stay consistent even when the baby is not.
- o Try to avoid ending every nap when they reach that twilight sleep stage 30-45 minutes in. Push at least two naps a day to 1½ hours.
- o **If** you get them up after 30-45 minutes, the hardest part may be keeping them awake until the next scheduled naptime so that the day and the baby stay on schedule.

SECTION FIVE: TYPICAL DAYS

Enjoying The Routine Of Family Life

"There is an appointed time for everything. And there is a time for every event under heaven."
Ecclesiastes 3:1

TYPICAL DAYS

"I just want to know what kind of schedule my baby should be on. I feel so lost."

Most babies thrive on a routine. However, the **times shown here are a guideline**. They represent the natural rhythms of a baby's day. Any of the following schedules can be moved in their entirety ½ hour earlier or later to adjust to your personal home schedule. (More options are available on the Moms on Call Scheduler App.)

We understand that schedules for modern parents need to be flexible. We also know that the babies who have regular nap times and feeding times tend to be more content. There is a delicate balance between being so scheduled that you cannot enjoy life and being so flexible that you cannot enjoy your baby.

This is a gradual process and not black and white. We do not want to overwhelm you with details. If one schedule is working for you and you are not ready to progress to the next, then stay with that one as long as it is working.

Every single day may not accommodate a schedule. That is why we included what we call "Crazy Day" guidelines, designated by a **(C*)** in the following schedules. These are the big things we want to try to keep solid in the schedule when nothing is going our way. That way you have a right hand line and a left hand line and you can settle anywhere in between.

You may feel like you take three steps forward and one step back. You may get them sleeping 8-hour stretches for a week and then one night, they are up at midnight. They all can have a bad night here or there, do not be discouraged.

It is our hope that these resources will meet the needs of the modern day family whether this is your first baby, set of babies or even your fourth child. Pay attention to as much detail as you find helpful.

The First Two Weeks
- Feed on demand every 2-3 hours from the **start** of one feeding to the **start** of the next.
- Feeding should not take any longer than 30-45 minutes start to finish, including burping (for both breast and bottle fed babies).
- Only spend about 2-3 minutes burping (do it ¾ of the way through the feeding and at the end).
- The most challenging part is keeping them awake: Scratch the bottoms of their feet, undress them down to the diaper or wipe their heads with a cool washcloth to help them stay awake for the feeding.
- Extend tons of grace—you are both just getting the hang of this. The first two weeks are a transition period for the whole family.

The following routines are for healthy babies who are gaining weight. (Babies with GI reflux are considered healthy as long as they are gaining weight).

TYPICAL DAY 2-4 WEEKS

*Breast or bottle feedings should take no longer than 30 minutes—start to finish. The bottle contains **3-4 ounces of breast milk or formula** unless otherwise noted.*

Between 6 and 7a.m.- Feed:

> *You can do the first feeding anytime between 6 and 7a.m. Then put them right back down in the crib to sleep. Feed at 6a.m. if the baby is awake, but if the baby is asleep then you can feed as late as 7a.m. Keep the rest of the schedule intact. May nap until next feeding.*

9 a.m.   (C*) Feed at this time regardless of when the baby ate last.

9:30 a.m.   Feeding is over and the next 10-30 minutes is playtime.

9:45/10 a.m.   Nap (as close to 2 hours as possible)

12 noon   Feed, even if you have to wake the baby.

12:30 p.m.   Feeding is over and the next 10-30 minutes is playtime.

12:45/1 p.m.   Nap (as close to 2 hours as possible)

3 p.m.   Feed, even if you have to wake the baby. The baby is generally alert and fussier than in the morning.

3:30 p.m.   Feeding is over and the next 10-30 minutes is playtime.

3:45/4 p.m.	Nap (as close to 2 hours as possible)
6 p.m.	**(C*)** "Supper Feed" If the clock says 6:00 p.m., then there is a breast or bottle in the baby's mouth. After this, do not feed again until 9 p.m.
6:30 p.m.	Feeding is over. The baby is increasingly fussy. We can do 5 minutes in the bouncy, 5 minutes of tummy time and then 5 minutes in the swing.
6:45/7 p.m.	May sleep for an hour to an hour and a half. May be increasingly fussy.
8:30 p.m.	**(C*)** Begin bath time routine (See "Bathing" section)
9 p.m.	**(C*)** Begin "Bedtime Feeding"
9:30 p.m.	Swaddle, put in crib, turn on white noise, and make sure the room is dark. (May let the baby cry for 2-5 minutes. Try increasing that time as they get older.)

Sometime between 12 a.m. and 2 a.m.

- See pages 110-111 for detailed instructions on feeding in the middle of the night.
- Feed in their room—keep it boring.
- Always wait 3-5 minutes before soothing and do this at least three times to ensure the baby is awake and hungry.
- Only count the time that the baby is truly crying—do not count whining, grunting or straining.
- Once fed, try to make it until 6 a.m. for the next feeding. Then start at the top.

C* -Crazy Day Tips

- o Try to feed at 9 a.m. each day.
- o No matter what happens during the day if we can meet the following two criteria then we can salvage our nighttime sleep.
  - o No naps last longer than 2.5 hours.
  - o Supper is a 6 p.m. (even if we have to scrunch two feedings together to get there).
- o If they do not eat really well at 6 p.m., then that last nighttime feeding at 9 p.m. will be fantastic and they will sleep really well. That helps us to keep 3 hours between supper and bedtime feedings.

Try to put the baby in the crib, swaddled with the white noise on for a minimum of 2 naps a day. That is where they will get their best rest. You can allow a little bit of sunlight into the room to help regulate that natural distinction between daytime and nighttime sleep. For more instructions on naptimes, see chapter entitled "Naptime."

The next schedule is exactly the same as this one except we moved supper and bedtime feedings a ½ hour earlier (5:30 p.m. and 8:30 p.m. respectively). What we found is that sleep does not shift, instead it expands. So, if we start getting the baby to bed a little earlier, they will sleep longer.

TYPICAL DAY 4-8 WEEKS

*Breast or bottle feedings should take no longer than 30 minutes—start to finish. The bottle contains **4-6 ounces of breast milk or formula** unless otherwise noted.*

Between 6 and 7 a.m.

> *You can do the first feeding anytime between 6 and 7 a.m. Feed at 6 a.m. if the baby is awake but if the baby is asleep then you can feed as late as 7 a.m. Keep the rest of the schedule intact. After this feed, they may nap in the crib or have low-key awake time in the bouncy seat until the 9 a.m. feeding.*

9 a.m.	**(C*)** Feed at this time regardless of when the baby ate last.
9:30 a.m.	Feeding is over and the next 10-30 minutes is playtime.
10 a.m.	Nap (as close to 2 hours as possible)
12 noon	Feed, even if you have to wake the baby.
12:30 p.m.	Feeding is over and the next 10-30 minutes is playtime.
1 p.m.	Nap (as close to 2 hours as possible)
3 p.m.	Feed, even if you have to wake the baby. The baby is generally alert and fussier than in the morning.
3:30 p.m.	Feeding is over and the next 10-30 minutes is playtime.

4 p.m.	Nap (may be closer to 1 ½ hours)
5:30 p.m.	**(C*)** "Supper Feed" If the clock says 5:30 p.m. then there is a breast or bottle in the baby's mouth. After this, do not feed again until 8:30 p.m.
6 p.m.	Feeding is over. The baby is increasingly fussy. We can do 5 minutes in the bouncy, 5 minutes on the activity mat and 5 minutes in the swing.
6:30 p.m.	May sleep for 45 min. to an hour and a half. May be increasingly fussy.
8 p.m.	**(C*)** Begin bath time routine. (See "Bathing" section.)
8:30 p.m.	**(C*)** Begin "Bedtime Feeding."
9 p.m.	Swaddle very well, put in crib, turn on white noise, and make sure the room is dark. (May let the baby cry for 5-8 minutes. Try increasing that time as they get older.)

Sometime between 2 a.m. and 3 a.m.:

- See pages 110-111 for detailed instructions on feeding in the middle of the night.
- We can wait 5-8 minutes before soothing and do this at least three times to ensure the baby is awake and hungry.
- If they fall back asleep, you do not have to wake them to feed them in the middle of the night.
- Try to make it until 6:30 or 7 a.m. for the next feeding using the above guidelines. Then start at the top.

C* -Crazy Day Tips
- o Try to feed at 9 a.m. each day
- o No matter what happens during the day if we can meet these two criteria then we can salvage our nighttime sleep.
  - o No naps last longer than 2 hours.
  - o Supper is a 5:30 p.m. (even if we have to scrunch two feedings together to get there).
- o If they do not eat really well at 5:30 p.m. then that last nighttime feeding at 8:30 p.m. will be fantastic and they will sleep really well. That helps us to keep 3 hours between supper and bedtime feedings.

Try to put the baby in the crib, swaddled with the white noise on for a minimum of 2 naps a day. That is where they will get their best rest. You can allow a little bit of sunlight into the room to help regulate that natural distinction between daytime and nighttime sleep. For more instructions on naptimes, see chapter entitled "Naptime."

Healthy babies that are gaining weight can move to the next schedule as early as 6 weeks of age! That means they sleep longer, sooner. What we found is that sleep does not shift, instead it expands. So if we start getting the baby to bed a little earlier, they will sleep longer.

TYPICAL DAY 8-16 WEEKS

*Breast or bottle feedings should take no longer than 20 minutes. The bottle contains 5-7 **ounces of breast milk or formula** unless otherwise noted. (Healthy babies that are gaining weight can transfer to this schedule as early as 6 weeks; just start naps about 15 minutes earlier than listed).*

7 a.m.   (C*) Feed, then awake and playful until the first nap.

8:30 a.m.   Nap (as close to 1½ hours as possible)

10 a.m.   Feed, then awake and playful until the nap.

11:30 a.m.   Nap (as close to 1½ hours as possible)

1 p.m.   Feed, the baby is generally alert and playful with on and off fussiness.

2:30 p.m.   Nap (as close to 1½ hours as possible)

4 p.m.   (C*) "Supper Feed" If the clock says 4 p.m. then there is a breast or bottle in the baby's mouth. After this, do not feed again until 7 p.m.

5:30 p.m.   Catnap (45 minutes – 1 hour) This catnap begins to get difficult and can be done in the swing (strapped in) if needed.

6:30 p.m.   (C*) Begin bath time routine

7 p.m.   (C*) "Bedtime Feeding"

| 7:30 p.m. | Put in crib, turn on white noise, and make sure the room is dark. Swaddle at night until 3 months of age or the baby is breaking out regularly—then see sleep section entitled "Sleep 3-6 months" |

Now we are likely to get past 4 a.m. (or even 5 a.m.).

- Under 3 months of age: See pages 110-111 for detailed instructions about backing up any middle of the night feedings. When they wake in the night, wait the three 5-10 minute sessions (30 minutes maximum) before feeding.
- 3 months and over: see the sleep section entitled "Sleep 3-6 months".

C* -Crazy Day Tips

- Try to feed at 7 a.m. each day.
- No matter what happens during the day if we can meet these two criteria then we can salvage our nighttime sleep.
    - No naps last longer than 2 hours.
    - Supper is a 4 p.m. (even if we have to scrunch 2 feedings together to get there).
- If they do not eat really well at the 4 p.m. feeding, then that last nighttime feeding at 7 p.m. will be fantastic and they will sleep really well. That helps us to keep 3 hours between supper and bedtime feedings.

TYPICAL DAY 4-6 MONTHS
(once baby foods are introduced)*

(The <u>bottle</u> contains 6-8 ounces and the <u>sippy cup</u> will contain 2-4 ounces of breast milk or formula unless otherwise noted. Baby food amounts do not really matter; we show amounts because parents want an idea of what is typical.)

7 a.m.   (C*) Wakes up; drinks formula/breast milk

8 a.m.   ½ jar fruit, 1-2 tablespoons of baby cereal. May begin to give sippy cup.

9 a.m.   Naptime 1-1 ½ hours

11 a.m.   Formula/breast milk

12 p.m.   2-4 oz. veggies, 2-4 oz. fruit, 1-2 tablespoons of baby cereal – Introducing a sippy cup here is fine.

12:30/1:30   Nap -pick one time between 12:30 and 1:30 and start nap at that time each day (ideally 1 ½-2 hours)

3 p.m.   Breast milk/formula

4 p.m.   2-4 oz. veggies, 2-4 oz. of fruit with a sippy cup of formula/breast milk

5 p.m.   May take a catnap.

6 p.m.   Keep awake from now until bath time. (Do 10 min. of tummy time—release that energy!)

6:30 p.m.   (C*) Start bath time routine

7 p.m.   (C*) Breastfeed or bottle feed

7:30 p.m.   (C*) In the crib for the night

- *See the chapter entitled "Sleep 3-6 months" if your baby is still waking in the middle of the night to feed*

C* -Crazy Day Tips

- o Try to feed at 7 a.m. each day.
- o No naps last longer than 2 hours.
- o We do not have to do three baby food feedings every day. If you just cannot make that happen (moms with multiple children) that is fine, just skip a baby food feeding and they will eat well at the next breast or formula feeding.
- o We just want the baby to be somewhat hungry at the "Bedtime Feeding" at 7 p.m. This will help them to get a good feeding before bed and sleep well.

*If not starting baby foods at 4 months of age, you can either stay on the 8-16 week schedule or use this 4-6 month schedule and skip the solids. That said, we REALLY recommend starting baby foods at 4 months of age.

Need help starting baby foods? Download our FREE Printable Baby Food Introduction Calendar at momsoncall.com.

Remember, the swaddle should be removed at nighttime around 3 months of age (see the chapter entitled *"Sleep 3-6 months – including dropping the swaddle")*. So, by 4 months of age, we should not be swaddling at any time. They are developmentally capable of finding their own comfy spot.

SECTION SIX: SAFETY

Ways To Keep Your Baby Safe

"I will lift my eyes to the hills - from whence comes my help? My help comes from the Lord, who made heaven and earth.
Psalm 121:1-2

IMMUNIZATIONS

"Can I give my baby acetaminophen before his immunizations to help it not hurt as much?"

Acetaminophen will not take away the pain of the actual injection. As a matter of fact, the baby will have forgotten the incident by the time you walk out the door (it will probably take *you* much longer to forget). We all get through it. We hate it, but we do get through it.

Site
- Given in thighs or arms.
- May be red and/or swollen for 2-3 days at site of injections.
- May have small pea-sized knots for several weeks after discoloration resolves.

Fever
- Fever 101°F up to 103.5°F rectally is expected for up to 24 hours after the immunizations are given (with the exception of the 12 month immunizations).
- Acetaminophen may be given every 4 hours according to the baby's weight. See your pediatrician's handout or website.

When to seek medical care
- Temp over 103.5° F rectally
- Fever over 101.5° F rectally that lasts more than 24 hours after immunizations were administered
- Crying inconsolably for 2 hours

- o Seizure activity (uncontrollable shaking)
- o Signs of allergic reaction (very rare) generally will happen within the first 15-20 minutes after administration of immunizations.:
  - o Difficulty breathing
  - o Wheezing
  - o Hives
  - o Pale and clammy
  - o Difficulty swallowing

Moms on Call LLC is in favor of vaccinating children. It is what the American Academy of Pediatrics recommends. Although the MMR (Measles Mumps and Rubella) vaccine is not administered until one year of age, you may have heard about studies linking the MMR vaccine with autism. This study has been completely debunked and retracted. More information is available at cdc.gov.

This much we **do** know: Prior to the MMR vaccination, over 100,000 children a year died of these combined diseases. If your child does not get immunized and contracts one of these diseases, it puts them and other children at risk, especially children under one year who have not yet been vaccinated.

The types of vaccinations that your child will get at 2, 4 and 6 months generally include:
- o DTP (Tetanus Diptheria Pertussis)
- o IPV (Injectable Polio Vaccine)
- o Prevnar (Protects against a bacteria that can cause meningitis and pneumonia)
- o HIB (Haemophilus B Influenzae - another bacteria that can cause meningitis)
- o Hep B (Hepatitis B - a disease of the liver transmitted through the blood and body

fluids of infected carriers)

Some of these immunizations are combined in one shot, so the most your child should get at one time is four shots; two in one thigh, two in the other. It is over very quickly.

After immunizations the baby is generally a little sleepier for 3-4 hours, then possibly fussy for the next 4-6. You can take the Band-Aids® off after about an hour.

Note: In the summertime, especially when baby's legs are exposed, they may try to pull off the Band-Aid® and eat it. Watch carefully!

12-15 month vaccinations generally include:
- o Varivax (Chicken Pox vaccine), if your child has not had the actual chicken pox yet
- o MMR (Measles, Mumps, and Rubella) Three diseases with rash and/or cough. Any of these diseases can be fatal.
- o These shots can go in the fatty tissue behind the arm or the fatty tissue in the thighs.

The 12-month vaccinations have side effects that are different from other immunizations. The **MMR** can cause a fever of up to 102.5°F rectally from 7-14 days after the immunization was given. It can also produce a pink pin-prickly rash that blanches with pressure on the torso and face. If your baby experiences these symptoms, call your pediatrician and remind them that your baby had immunizations 1-2 weeks ago. These side effects are not dangerous and resolve on their own in about 48 hours from the time they began. The baby is also generally playful and alert throughout the extent of the symptoms.

The **Varivax** vaccine can produce a rash that looks like small pus-filled bumps that generally starts on the abdomen. These bumps are only contagious 20% of the time and only to people who have not had chicken pox and **only** if they were exposed to the pus inside the bumps. This rash should also resolve on its own in 4-5 days.

15-18 month vaccinations generally include:
- DTP (Tetanus, Diptheria, Pertussis)
- IPV (Injectable Polio Vaccine)
- HIB (Haemophilus B Influenzae - another bacteria that can cause meningitis)
- Possibly Prevnar (which protects against a bacteria that can cause meningitis and pneumonia)

CHILDPROOFING/SAFETY

Childproofing: Accidents are just that—ACCIDENTS. However, there are measures that we can take to minimize our child's risk. According to the American Heart Association, injuries are the leading cause of death in children and young adults. Childproofing and being knowledgeable about possible hazards can help you minimize that risk for your child.

We cannot stress enough the importance of taking regular CPR training. The question you should ask yourself and your child's caretakers is not only, "When did you take your last CPR class?" but more importantly, "If my child were choking or unresponsive, would I know what to do?" (Yes, we know that you said "Call 911" in your head, but there are life saving steps that you can take while 911 is on the way!)

Please, please, please, know what to do if your child is choking. CPR classes are offered through the American Heart Association and the Red Cross. Almost all area hospitals offer regular classes.

Common Safety Issues. Here is a quick but not exhaustive checklist for some common safety issues.

- Put outlet protectors for outlets not being used and an outlet cover attachment that can be used on outlets that *are* being used. Children will try to play with cords that are plugged in.
- Keep blind cords short and out of reach of children.
- Check the safety of the crib. Slats should be no wider than 2 3/8 inches apart. There should be no more than 2 inches between the mattress edges and the crib.
- Do not put any pillows, stuffed animals or anything in the bed. If you think your child needs more warmth, use a sleeper (fleece zip-up).

Bathroom
- Always unplug any appliances to avoid electric shock.
- Set hot water heater to 120 degrees Fahrenheit. Always check temperature of water before placing child in it.
- Always empty water out of the bathtub immediately after using it.
- Put non-skid bath mats on bottom of tub.
- NEVER LEAVE YOUR CHILD UNATTENDED IN THE BATH FOR ANY REASON FOR ANY LENGTH OF TIME! This means if the phone rings, let it ring! They can leave a message.

Kitchen
- Avoid tablecloths. They can be pulled down with hot food sliding onto baby's head. (As a child, Laura pulled a tablecloth and a pot of hot grits

fell on her foot. The burn marks are still there.)
- Always be aware of where your child is when transporting hot foods or liquids.
- HOUSE RULE: NO toys on the kitchen floor. You can trip and drop hot liquid on kids.

Living Area
- Be aware of windows. These should have safety locks so they can only be opened a few inches. (May be purchased at home improvement stores.)
- Check all furniture to see if it falls over easily, especially bookcases. Where *we* see a bookcase, a little boy sees a ladder. Anchor your bookcases to the wall. (Trust me, Bryce loved to try this—Jennifer).
- Keep electrical cords out of reach. TV cord can be pulled and cause the TV to come crashing down on a child's head.
- Never leave your child alone with pets.
- Always check stair railing for sturdiness.

Choking
Liquid that is swallowed at meals will usually clear itself in 10-30 seconds.

Solids:
- If the child is coughing vigorously and can talk and breathe, then do nothing. Do not slap a child on the back who may be choking when they are in the upright position. This can lodge the foreign object in the throat.
- Removal of a foreign object is best learned in a CPR class.
- Do not put your fingers in the child's mouth

unless you see an object. Only then can you perform a finger sweep of the mouth.

Car Seats

- It is best to have your car seat checked by a professional. Some local fire departments will also check your installation; call first to see which location near you offer this service. Many times, this requires an appointment.
- Your car seat will come with weight limits. Check the side and back for information on placement and weight requirements.
- Check with your state's department of motor vehicles to get current guidelines.
- Straps need to be snug. The front clip should be at the nipple line and no more than two of your fingers should fit between the strap and your child. Again, note the manufacturer's guidelines. If you have any questions, see a checkpoint near you.
- When tightening the seat in the car, put your knee in the base of the car seat. Then thread the seatbelt through the car seat according to manufacturer's guidelines. The seat should move no more than ½ inch from side to side. Always remember to use the additional safety clip (often sold separately) to clip to the seatbelt. The safest place to put a car seat is in the middle of the back seat. Never put a child under 12 years old in the front seat of a car with an airbag. The airbag can deploy with such force that it instantly kills a child. **Never put the car seat in the front seat of a car**.
- Many newer model cars come with a tether attachment in the rear of the vehicle. Tether equipment can also be purchased at most baby stores.

QUICK-GRAB FIRST AID KIT

"We are out of town and I think my baby has a fever but we forgot to bring a thermometer."

You will need the following items when you least expect it. Keep one in the car and one at home. These are to be kept out of the reach of children. We recommend buying a container with a handle and a lid. On the inside of the lid, list the pediatrician's number, emergency numbers and the number of Poison Control.

- o   Band-Aids®
- o   Children's acetaminophen
- o   Diphenhydramine
- o   Digital thermometer
- o   Hydrocortisone 0.5%
- o   Polysporin®
- o   Anti-bacterial wash
- o   Hydrogen peroxide
- o   Pack of 4x4 Gauze and 2x2 gauze
- o   Ace bandage
- o   Squeezable ice pack
- o   Tweezers
- o   Medical tape

POISONING

POISON CONTROL
404-616-9000 (Atlanta area)
1-800-222-1222 (other areas)

Always call your poison control center immediately if you think your child has swallowed a poison or other substance that they should not have had.

You will be asked the following:
- o What was swallowed?
- o How much? Always estimate the maximum amount.
- o How long ago was it swallowed?
- o What symptoms, if any, is the child showing now?
- o Age and approximate weight of child. Keep in mind that dads do not always get to go to visits to the pediatrician, and may not know what the child weighs. Post the child's most recent weight on your refrigerator.

Prevention
- o Keep all chemicals, medicines, and cleaners out of reach and locked!
- o Get a list from your local garden center or plant supplier of any poisonous house or outdoor plants. For example, holly berries are poisonous. Get rid of all poisonous houseplants.
- o Keep alcoholic beverages out of reach and locked.

CLOSING REMARKS

In the Moms on Call logo, you will find the words: Sleep, Feed, Laugh and Love. We want to talk about leading a balanced life filled with moments of sheer laughter and enjoyment. The entire purpose of this resource is to provide you with more time to actually enjoy your children.

Sleep
Families who enjoy healthy sleep habits are happy, content and have a stable foundation in which to handle the regular day-to-day challenges of life (not to mention drive a car without being bleary eyed!). All of the sleep instructions have a goal in mind—to transform stressed, sleep deprived families that are hanging on for dear life into well-rested, confident people who look forward to daytime *and* nighttime.

Feed
Feedings are a time of togetherness and sharing. We seek to take the stress out of this natural and normal part of life. If there is a perfect time to laugh and play together, then mealtime is one of our favorites.
If you do not know how to get from here to there, we have taken all the guesswork out for you.

Laugh
A healthy family life involves a good deal of laughter. **We need time to play with our children that is not "educational" time or "instructional" time.** Just dance, sing and enjoy being together. Freedom! Leave the

stress of the workday behind. We focus on household order so that we can take a break from the activities of daily life, slow down the hustle and bustle and just enjoy the intense blessing and laughter that children bring.

Love
We assume that you are reading this resource because you love your children and desire to really enjoy them. Love comes in many forms. Sometimes, love means that we will take on the uncomfortable decisions that we have to make in order to provide a clear structure for the household where our children live and thrive. Peppered throughout this resource, we have an overriding theme of support. Love means believing in our children's ability to do the things that life requires. We are dedicated to providing parents with trusted information so that families can make order out of chaos and love their time together.

Sleep, Feed. Laugh. Love
Moms on Call
Parenting the First Four Years.

At Moms on Call we hope that this resource has been a blessing to your household, given you greater confidence and ultimately helped you to have more time to enjoy life with your precious little ones.

NOTES

SLEEP · FEED

MOMS ON CALL

PARENTING THE FIRST 4 YEARS

LAUGH · LOVE

For more Moms On Call resources, please go to
www.momsoncall.com

More than 175,000 books sold:
Moms On Call: Basic Baby Care (0-6 months)
Moms On Call: Next Steps Baby Care (6-15 months)
Moms On Call: Toddler Book

PARENTING RESOURCES: NEWBORN - 4 YEARS OF AGE

Online Classes:
- Three comprehensive online courses
- Dozens of complimentary videos
- Available via multiple platforms to meet families where they are

One-on-One Consultations:
- In-home consultations
- Virtual consultations
- On-Going Email Support
- Network of Trained Consultants

Mobile Apps (IOS/Android):
- Moms On Call Scheduler
- Moms On Call Toddler by Design

Products:
- The Official Moms On Call Swaddle Blanket
- More to come!